fight back

Arm Yourself with Mental and Physical Self-Defense

by Dominick DiVito

with A. J. GREGORY

Foreword by Wynonna Judd

CENTER
STREET

NEW YORK • BOSTON • NASHVILLE

Copyright © 2005 by Summer Haven, Inc.

Foreword, copyright © 2005 by Wynonna Judd

Center Street
Time Warner Book Group
1271 Avenue of the Americas, New York, NY 10020
Visit our website at www.twbookmark.com

The Center Street name and logo are registered trademarks of the Time Warner Book Group.

Printed in the United States of America

First Edition: October 2005

10 9 8 7 6 5 4 3 2 1

Library of Congress Cataloging-in-Publication Data
DiVito, Dominick.
   Fight back : arm yourself with mental and physical self-defense / Dominick DiVito.—1st ed.
    p. cm.
  ISBN 1-931722-46-3
1. Self-defense—Handbooks, manuals, etc.   I. Title.
  GV1111.D56 2005
  613.6'6—dc22   2005014869

Book design by Victoria Hartman

RODNEY JONES

April 27, 1965 – July 9, 1986

This book is dedicated to Rodney Jones, the brother I never had. His influence will always be embedded in my heart. A once-in-a-lifetime friend, Rodney introduced the art of Kenpo to me. I vowed to him that I would never let our passion for Kenpo die, and that people would be safer through the passing of our knowledge. This book is a promise kept.

ACKNOWLEDGMENTS

Thank you to . . .

First, I want to thank my Lord and Savior Jesus Christ for making all things possible.

To my wife, Mary Lee—for being with me during the thick and thin, never letting me forget that you love me. You are my life.

To Dad and Mom and my entire family—for believing in me and supporting me and never giving up on my dream. No words describe my love for all of you.

To Dena—for being my partner since day one. Your love and wisdom has been my strength. Thank you for never giving up.

To the Jones family—for being such a special part of my life. You mean more to me than you will ever know.

To Esther—for seeing my passion to empower people. I thank you for your dedication.

To A. J.—for "getting it."

To Bill Murphy—for being not just my instructor, but also a man I respect and honor by keeping your art alive.

To Wynonna Judd—for supporting me and my goals and for being such a good friend.

To Christina Boys and everyone who helped out at Center Street—your hard work and dedication to this book is appreciated!

CONTENTS

FOREWORD

In 2000, after my divorce was final, I moved with my two children to a secluded house out in the country. I loved being in such a peaceful setting, but fear permeated my thoughts. Being alone, once again, left me, at times, vulnerable to my insecurities. What would I do if someone invaded our home? I did not want to purchase a gun because of my children, but I wanted peace of mind in knowing I could protect my family. I did not want to live in fear. I prayed for an answer; God responded with Dominick DiVito.

Through my self-defense training with Dominick, I am reclaiming my power, and I want to start a campaign across America to show people how they, too, can be stronger and claim victory in their lives. As a mother, I have gained peace of mind knowing how to protect my babies. I have replaced the feelings I once had of helplessness with self-empowerment. Thanks to Dominick, I now wake up every day and put on my armor of God and go out kicking and fighting. I feel more alive now than I ever did before.

Wynonna Judd
March 7, 2005

Part I

Mental Self-Defense

It *Can* Happen to You . . .
And You *Can* Do Something About It

There exists a law, not written down anywhere, but inborn in our hearts; a law which comes to us not by training or custom or reading . . . a law which has come to us not from theory but from practice, not by instruction but by natural intuition. I refer to the law which lays it down that, if our lives are endangered by plots or violence or armed robbers or enemies, any and every method of protecting ourselves is morally right.

—MARCUS TULLIUS CICERO, 44 BC

"Don't make a sound or I'll kill you . . . just do exactly what I say"—a ruthless command and a lethal threat on an innocent human being. It wasn't a statement coming through a television set from an episode of *Cops* or a Lifetime movie. Nor was it a practical joke carried out by one of her friends. It was real and it was happening to Caryn—a tall, thin, and ultra-feminine woman who had always thought with confidence, *It [rape] won't happen to me.* But there he was and there she was.

At ten o'clock that night, Caryn had checked that her doors were locked, as usual, before shutting the lights off and going to bed. She assumed she was safe within the protection of her apartment walls. A typical night coupled with a typical attitude. At four o'clock in the morning, the scene drastically changed. Her worst fear had crept out of her nightmares and forced its way into her bedroom. While she slept, a man had broken into her locked apartment and moved silently into her bedroom. He woke her from a peaceful sleep with the forceful words, "Don't make a sound, don't move." That statement would resonate in her mind for years. *Don't . . . don't . . . don't,* he was telling her, while he granted himself permission to violate her body any way he pleased.

This desperate, angry man—a man she'd never seen before in her life—stood over her in her bedroom and made one last reminder for her not to do anything. Caryn's mind raced back to my self-defense workshop, and she was reminded of the emphasis placed on fighting back in order to surprise the attacker. *Don't think of anything other than survival. Find the opportunity—it may be as little as five seconds—when he is vulnerable and use it to your advantage. Fight back.* And that is what she did. She knew she needed to remain calm, assess the best time for defense, and strike.

He pulled back the blankets that covered her and lifted a leg to climb on top of her as he started to unbuckle his belt. There he was, with only one foot on the floor, fingers clumsily fumbling with his pants. She recognized her opportunity and went for it. Bending her knees and thinking of nothing but survival, she kicked him in the chest with both of her feet, using all the force she could muster. As she watched his body fly across the room, Caryn was amazed to see the shock resonating on his face. He was caught so physically and mentally off-guard by her blow that she had enough time to escape. As she rushed out of her apartment to get help, he ran, too . . . not after her, but away from her.

You may be curious as to how the intruder managed to break into Caryn's apartment without her hearing any noises indicative of a break-in. The sad fact is that the man had a key from the tenant who'd previously lived in that apartment. Apparently, the landlord never changed the locks when Caryn moved in, and as a result of that negligence, Caryn experienced a life-threatening situation. It is our responsibility to ensure our own safety and that means, sometimes, making sure other people do their jobs.

Caryn was one of the students in my self-defense workshops, and she experienced this ordeal in September 1997. Luckily, she was prepared.

Would you have been prepared? I want to make sure that *you will be.*

Crime: It Exists

Violent crime is a national concern. More than half of Americans say reducing crime should be a top legislative priority, according to a report conducted by the Pew Research Center in January 2004. It wasn't long ago that parents were able to drop their kids off at school with a sigh of relief, knowing they would be safe inside. Today, with the incidence of school shootings and assaults, parents can only hope their school's security systems will serve to prevent another Columbine.

FAST FACTS

In 2003, for every one thousand people age twelve or older, there occurred:

- One rape or sexual assault.
- One assault with injury.
- Two robberies.

National Crime Victimization Survey
(Washington, DC: Bureau of Justice Statistics, 2003)

Being aware of the prevalence of crime throughout our country is the first step in building solid offenses and defenses against these monstrosities. When we put blinders over our eyes and remain apathetic toward current statistics and abundant media reports about criminal activity, we are doing a disservice to ourselves and those we love. In addition, being oblivious to crime creates a detrimental sense of inattentiveness. We are no longer aware of what is going on around us. We are dangerously boxed inside our idealistic worlds. Criminals love us; we make the best targets.

Mental and physical self-defense is about being smart, not being irrational or impractical. Obviously, there aren't attackers lurking in every single dark alley or parking garage in the world. Not every guy you date will try to rape you. Being aware means understanding the possibilities and being prepared should you face them one day.

While awareness is necessary to understand the danger of crime and determine measures of prevention, being educated in mental and physical self-defense is necessary to walk away from a deadly situation alive. Proper education in this powerful duo can be effective in surprising your attacker and, ultimately, crippling his power over your life. This book is designed to equip you with the mental and physical resources to combat an assailant, regardless of size, weight, and weapon possession.

Now . . . It's About *You!*

I'd like to give you my official congratulations! You have taken the first step necessary to learn mental and physical self-defense: You picked up **this book!** Just by reading these words, you have acknowledged the problem of crime and are looking to find a solution that will create a safer environment for you and the ones you love. More important, right before you started flipping through the pages of this book, you made another significant decision: You willingly created a conscious commitment to learn about self-defense. You have opted to empower yourself with knowledge rather than sitting on the sidelines and letting everyone else worry about safety. You made the wise choice to soak in this information, which has been compiled to keep you safer, make you more aware, and, ultimately, save your life.

But specifically, why? Why did you decide to read this book?

Focusing on and reminding ourselves of the reason or reasons we want to learn something is a great way to strengthen our commitment and solidify our desire to learn. So why did you pick up this book? Why are you really interested in learning about self-defense?

Below are some good reasons my students have shared with me as to why they wished to equip themselves with these lifesaving tools. Which of these do you relate most to?

- I'm a stay-at-home mom with two kids under the age of five and my husband works late most nights. I wouldn't know what to do if an intruder ever came in.
- I travel by myself a lot for my job. I want to be able to learn how to protect myself anywhere I go.
- I just don't know anything about self-defense and want to learn.
- I want to know how to protect my wife and children and not rely solely on my muscle power.
- I was once a victim and was unprepared. I don't want it to happen again.
- The thought of being raped frightens me.
- I don't want to become another statistic.
- I have three children and I don't know what they would do if something bad happened to me.
- I want to become more confident, wiser, more aware, and prepared should anything ever happen. I feel too afraid now.

Now what about you? On the next page, write down the top three reasons that have prompted you to learn about safety and self-defense. During the course of reading this book, refer back to these notes and remind yourself why you want to learn self-defense. It will help you to focus on your specific needs and reinforce what you will learn.

Why I Want to Learn Self-Defense

1. _To stay safe and protect myself_

2. _Be fit, strong and healthy_

3. _take more confidence and be a BADASS!_

Additionally, when you have read the final page of this book, come right back to this section and see if what you have learned has satisfied what you wrote down. Do you feel more mentally empowered? Are you confident you can physically defend yourself? Are you more aware of your surroundings?

On the other hand, I'm sure you have a plethora of thoughts as to some challenges that you either anticipate or are currently facing when it comes to self-defense. Maybe you think you're too old. Or too young. Or too weak, small, tall, fat, skinny, or tired. Perhaps you are wondering whether or not you could actually defend yourself if the need ever arose. I'm sure you want to learn how to execute self-defense, but you might feel a slight skepticism in your overall ability.

Not a problem! In working with both male and female students for twenty-plus years, I'm pretty confident I've heard it all. Most people walk into self-defense workshops with questions, concerns, and even fears! Learning anything for the first time can be challenging, and we usually carry some predetermined opinions and thoughts with us at the very beginning of the process. When I train my students for the first time, they address their concerns with me about learning self-defense. These include:

- Just look at me, Dominick, I'm five feet tall and weigh a hundred pounds! How can I defend myself against someone twice my size?
- I'm the most uncoordinated person alive. There is no way I can perform these techniques.
- I'm too scared; I can't even hurt a fly!
- Does self-defense *really* work?

Let's get back to you again. Take a few moments and think of the top three challenges you are facing right now as you begin the journey to learn self-defense. Another effective way to get the most out of learning something is by admitting initial concerns and apprehensions. Be honest with yourself by speaking about what seems to bother you and then take the appropriate steps to overcome those things. What's going on in your head at this very moment? Are you worried you are too weak to defend against a bigger person? Are you afraid you might freeze up at the moment you should be doing the opposite? List your challenges below.

Challenges I Might Face

1. *Physical weakness, Coordination*
   fear response
   Arthritis
2. *SHAME AND PAIN*
   Being hurt and / or killed
3. *Skill SET*

Once again, when you are finished reading this book, review the challenges you mentioned above. I'm sure they will have been conquered through acquired knowledge and through developing a strong, confident attitude!

Get Ready to Learn!

This book was written for you as an empowering resource to make you feel self-assured in defending yourself. Through reading the subsequent chapters, you will specifically learn:

- Tips to create the safest environment possible wherever you are.
- How to be aware and present at all times.
- The importance of self-confidence and self-worth.
- Why you need both the mental and physical aspects of self-defense.
- The motivations and behaviors of criminals and what they look for in their victims.
- How to fight an attacker's weaknesses, not his strengths.

Unfortunately, it seems that everyone always wants to get to the good stuff first. They want to learn how to throw a punch or take a man or woman down, and they want to learn it *now*. Most of us who have taken music lessons as a child have experienced the boredom and annoyance of learning theory prior to playing the real songs. Still, we understand that training in theoretical exercises and scales will provide the right foundation for playing fun songs. Learning the basics is what is necessary in order to ultimately sound good.

It's the same with self-defense. Before we can start to play pretend victim and throw our peers on a mat in a smelly gym, we need to recognize the significant role of the mind. A certain mental attitude needs to be established well before physical techniques can be learned. The first part of this book focuses on the things we all need to understand before we learn how we can physically defend ourselves.

The second part of this book delves primarily into the physical aspect of it all. My approach is scenario-driven. The scenarios I use are taken from the various workshops I have taught and the many conversations I've had with students about their most feared situations. You must keep in mind that every scenario is unique in and of itself and variables always change.

You *Can* Do It!

Let's begin this journey by exposing the common myths about self-defense that may be on some of your minds. I'll uncover the truth through statistics, facts, and common sense.

You are now on your way to living a safer life!

2

Fact Versus Fiction:
Debunking the Myths of Self-Defense

*No greater wrong can ever be done than to put a good man at the mercy of a
bad, while telling him not to defend himself or his fellows; in no way can
the success of evil be made surer or quicker.*

—THEODORE ROOSEVELT

We've all got excuses for at least one thing in our life that we don't do or,
alternatively, spend too much time doing. *I can't keep my house clean because I
have no time. I can't quit smoking because it's the only thing that de-stresses me. I can't
go on antidepressant medication because it will change me into a different person!*
While there may be some element of truth to these statements, ultimately
they serve as groundless deterrents preventing us from following through
with the intended action and reaping the benefits.

A special thing can happen when you begin to truly understand or directly experience the consequences born of your excuses and inaction:
You get a really good reality check. This reality check usually predicates
an automatic change in your way of thinking.

The use of antidepressants, for example, used to have an enormous
social stigma that has since decreased. Years ago, if you mentioned the
word *Prozac*, people might have thought *funny farm, crazy*, or a multitude of
other negative ideas. Today, those who suffer from acute depression and
are prescribed an antidepressant are educated by their physician as to the

benefits and side effects. This is done to dispel any myths the patients have that might prevent them from taking the medication. Some might be initially hesitant for fear of what others might think; others might worry about becoming addicted. Still others may think of it as a "happy pill" that will completely alter their moods and personalities. But through years of research, clinical studies, and trials, we know that antidepressants are simply used to balance chemical levels in the brain. They will not turn anyone into a completely perky, carefree person, nor into an apathetic, comatose one. Becoming educated makes a person more understanding, more aware, and, essentially, more comfortable with the truth.

This myth concept has the same influence in the self-defense world. There are many myths out there that make people apprehensive toward or opposed to self-defense. You may notice I interchange the words *myth* and *excuse* in this chapter, because a myth can be—and often is—used as an excuse for not doing something. There are both simplistic and false beliefs running rampant throughout our culture that prevent safety awareness and personal self-defense. My purpose in this chapter is to uncover these myths, correct them with the truth, and make you see the importance and ultimate necessity of learning how to protect yourself.

Some of the general fallacies out there regarding self-defense may achieve the following negative objectives:

- They can undermine your awareness of the necessity and effectiveness of self-defense.
- They may link self-defense in your mind with negative characteristics, such as hostility, aggression, arrogance, or violence.
- They can cause you to underestimate the mental and physical abilities possessed by every human being that can prevent or de-escalate an attack.
- They can make you ignorant of the actual possibility that you can be a victim.

- They may deny you the God-given right to defend yourself or your property.

FAST FACTS

In 2003, 53 percent of incidents of violent crime occurred during the day, between 6 AM and 6 PM.

National Crime Victimization Survey
(Washington, DC: Bureau of Justice Statistics, 2003)

What happens when we logically try to understand the objectives, effectiveness, and techniques of self-defense? Simple. We can save our lives or the life of someone we love. We can prevent ourselves from becoming a statistic of crime. Imagine that! While learning self-defense does not guarantee a free pass away from crime, your chances of survival are significantly increased.

By educating yourself, here's what happens: Your level of awareness is heightened, your intuition is fine-tuned, and your physical abilities are honed so that your chances of being raped, attacked, or even murdered are statistically lessened. You won't walk down a certain street when instinct kicks in and tells you to turn back. When someone grabs you from behind, your immediate reaction to freeze will turn into an action to fight back. You will begin to see that a seemingly hopeless and defenseless situation has more opportunities for defense than you could have ever imagined.

So how about those myths?!

Myth #1: *I own a gun and that is the best possible method of self-defense. If someone attacks me, I can use it to protect myself.*

Fact #1: Well, congratulations! I use that sarcasm because I've often heard this statement repeated with a cavalier attitude, as if owning a gun is the only sufficient method of self-defense. Don't get me wrong: Weapons are definitely advantageous and necessary when situations demand their use. If you were in charge of the Department of Defense, I'm confident you wouldn't equip a troop of U.S. Marines headed to the Middle East with bottles of pepper spray, really loud whistles, and butter knives. It is critical to arm these soldiers during battle with top-of-the-line deadly weapons in order to fulfill their obligations, specifically to be able to fight offensively and defensively during wartime. That is good common sense.

Now, I do support the constitutional amendment giving American citizens the right to bear arms. If you wake up in the middle of the night hearing strange noises clearly indicative of a burglar pillaging your good china and God-knows-what-else, having a gun nestled safely in your night table is a good thing. You probably have just enough time to (1) make a quick 911 call; (2) retrieve your weapon; and (3) muster up enough courage to head toward the direction of the burglar and attempt to intimidate and stall him until the police arrive. A gun is a handy piece of equipment when used with knowledge, good judgment, and respect. More important, it's best if you have the time to use it.

Realistically speaking, though, when you are attacked by a criminal, it happens without warning. You are not given even a tiny margin of time to prepare your defensive actions. I don't care if you own a rifle the size of Wal-Mart or a samurai sword that would tickle Tom Cruise pink. You are not going to be afforded the time necessary to pull out and use your weapon of choice. For example, let's say you are walking out of your local mall and are unexpectedly pushed to the ground by a teenage thug brandishing a pistol. Even if you have a hand grenade tucked away in your pocketbook, it's not going to help the situation. When faced with predicaments that call for immediate self-defense, only two things are readily available—your mind and your body. That's it.

I'm not saying a gun isn't useful in certain situations or as a means of intimidation; I'm saying that the odds of being able to access a weapon in enough time so that it retains its benefits are pretty slim. A gun in your safety-deposit box at home won't help you when someone attacks you while you're jogging in the park. Learn how to use yourself as a weapon and you might not have to worry about owning a gun. This same principle applies to any weapons—including knives, pepper spray, or Mace.

Myth #2: *Self-defense will only make me masculine, aggressive, and hostile. I don't want to become a GI Jane–type woman!*

Fact #2: Most women don't want to be known as brutes, raging fighting machines, or ruthless warriors—this I understand. Self-defense in the pure form does convey a sense of aggression in its call to physically fight back. However, there is a time and a place for everything. If a stranger walked up to you in a grocery store and, for absolutely no reason, slapped your cheek, you wouldn't respond by politely smiling and curiously inquiring why he slapped you. You would probably want to slap him back and use some colorful, choice words in the process. This does *not* mean you have a hostile temperament; you are simply responding to the situation.

You also must use self-defense for the right reasons. If you're learning self-defense because you want to kick some butt, you're doing it for the wrong reasons and you will, likely, become more hostile and aggressive. Negative feelings are created from negative motives. If you're walking to your car in a deserted parking lot late at night and cross the path of someone who merely looks suspicious in your eyes, would you haul off and punch him just in case? I hope not. Self-defense is a way to learn awareness and reactionary self-protection measures.

A study conducted by the University of Washington in 1997 backs my thoughts. It included data contradicting ill-conceived notions that self-defense promotes aggression and hostility. Ronald Smith, a UW psychology professor and coauthor of the study, remarked,

> People who feel vulnerable often use hostility and violence to protect themselves. They almost adopt the attitude that "the best defense is a good offense." However, the women in this study who learned martial arts techniques of aikido and karate reported feeling more assertive, but less hostile and aggressive.

Myth #3: *It won't happen to me. I live, work, and hang out in a good neighborhood. I am not statistically or geographically likely to experience crime.*

Fact #3: This myth suggests that crime victims are always in the wrong place at the wrong time. Let's take a look at cold, hard facts.

FAST FACTS

Every 22.8 seconds, one violent crime occurs:

- One aggravated assault every 36.8 seconds.
- One robbery every 1.3 minutes.
- One forcible rape every 5.6 minutes.
- One murder every 31.8 minutes.

Every 3.0 seconds, one property crime occurs:

- One larceny-theft every 4.5 seconds.
- One burglary every 14.6 seconds.
- One motor vehicle theft every 25 seconds.

Crime Clock
(Washington, DC: Federal Bureau of Investigation, 2003)

According to the statistics researched and published by the U.S. Department of Justice, there were more than twenty-two million victims of some type of crime in 2003. Do you believe that all these folks were aimlessly walking around in sleazy neighborhoods, putting themselves in vulnerable situations, or subconsciously inviting crime into their lives? Were all of these victims at the wrong place at the wrong time? Or do bad things happen, sometimes, for reasons that are unknown and in situations that are out of our control? Most of us live in our own little imaginary worlds where unspeakable things don't exist. Most people don't think that anything dreadful will happen to them, whether it be a serious car accident, a fatal disease, divorce, or a really bad perm. It's always someone else . . . someone else's daughter, wife, or husband. But if we live life long enough—say, past age fifteen—it becomes apparent that things don't always go our way and stuff (to use a softer word) happens.

The fact is, one in every six women in the United States is the victim of attempted or completed rape. Surely you know five other women beside yourself. One of you has been or is likely to get raped. Now, if that doesn't concern you, it should, at the very least, give you something to think about.

The sad part of the *it-won't-happen-to-me* mentality is that it is uselessly ingrained in our minds until something terrible happens. And at that point, it's too late. When we don't raise our level of awareness and make appropriate offensive and defensive provisions, we run the risk of being sucker-punched.

Here's an example. Obesity is on the rise. If you're not currently obese, I'm confident you don't want to become a part of the statistics. So what are reasonable things to do? Eat less and exercise more. You try to prevent something like obesity from happening by taking these logical measures. In the self-defense world, you can try to prevent yourself from becoming a rape, burglary, or homicide statistic by paying more attention to your surroundings and learning how to protect yourself should the unfortunate occur. This is the same reason most states demand that automobile owners purchase car insurance. You never know what might happen—but should the worst occur, you'd better be prepared.

Myth #4: *Fighting back will only make things worse.*

Fact #4: True, with fighting back there is a chance that your actions will make your attacker more angry, determined, or violent than he was before you decided to defend yourself. On the other hand, if a person is

---

FAST FACTS

According to the 2002 *National Crime Victimization Survey,* approximately 60 percent of criminal victims took some measure of self-protection. Here is a breakdown of the effectiveness of self-defense noted in these cases:

- 64.8 percent said it helped the situation.
- 9.7 percent said it hurt the situation.
- 4.9 percent said it both helped and hurt the situation.
- 11.8 percent said it neither helped nor hurt the situation.
- 8.2 percent said they didn't know.
- In 0.6 percent of the cases, information wasn't available.

Of the victimizations in which self-protective measures taken by the victim were helpful:

- 46.3 percent avoided injury.
- 15.3 percent scared the offender(s).
- 16.6 percent escaped the situation.
- 5.2 percent protected property.
- 6.5 percent protected others.
- 9.4 percent helped in other ways.
- In 0.6 percent of the cases, information wasn't available.

intent on violating you in some way, shape, or form, what will happen? He will rape you anyway. Or he will kill you anyway. Or he will kidnap your child before your eyes. So the question remains: What risk are you willing to take? The simple fact is that doing nothing is the worst thing to do.

I am not egotistical or stupid enough to tell you that defending yourself is a guarantee that you will walk away the victor. But I can guarantee that you stand a much better chance of survival if you do *something* rather than nothing.

The best possible result you can achieve from using self-defense is that you will walk away alive. The worst result is that the criminal will do to you whatever he intended in the first place. This is obviously a chance worth taking!

Myth #5: *I'm too busy. I don't have time to learn self-defense.*

Fact #5: Don't you love playing the busy card? This excuse can be used across the proverbial board, from canceling social engagements, to researching better car insurance, to exercising, to absolutely anything! And the reason is that we Americans truly are busy. We have kids, we have jobs, we have household work, we have social obligations, we exercise, we read the paper, we watch TV! Watch TV?

I've often asked people how much TV they watch a day. The response typically is, "Oh, not much at all, maybe an hour or so. I mainly watch the news or learn things on the History or Discovery Channel." Hmmm . . . really? In 2003, the U.S. Bureau of Labor Statistics reported in the *American Time Use Survey* that the average man watched 2.7 hours of TV per day, and the average woman 2.4 hours. Let's be realistic: Statistically speaking, are we spending two and a half hours of our day watching CNN or learning about the Cold War?

I'm not saying TV is bad, I'm merely suggesting we may be spending a little too much time being entertained by this addictive box. It's one way we can add some extra hours to our day. I know, I know, there are many of you reading this right now who may be filled with indignation. *Dominick*, you might say, *I don't watch three hours of TV a day. That's silly! It's impossible when I put in sixty hours of work at the office.* Yes, I understand. But I am speaking in generalities. Statistics show most of us watch too much TV. Most, not all. I mention this so you can carefully evaluate how you spend your time. There are other activities we engage in that we may not need to spend so much time doing. If we were all honest with ourselves, there are key areas in our daily routines that we can spend less time on.

How much time does it really take to learn self-defense? Minimally speaking, there are a couple of basic techniques you can learn to save your life. The optimal form of self-defense training is where you can attend a class, about once a week for a few weeks, that focuses on survival training rather than exclusively martial arts techniques. Additionally, it will behoove you to spend a few minutes a day practicing these techniques. But just learning the basics of self-defense doesn't require taking a five-week course and doesn't have to consume a majority of your time. You can learn them in about an hour with a good training course, or, I hope, by reading this book.

Finally, yes, we all lead busy lives. But if we're dead or incapacitated to some degree because of a crime that we may have been able to prevent, we won't have our lives to decide how we spend our time. It's as simple as that. Will learning self-defense take time? Sure, but ultimately it's time well spent.

Myth #6: *My boyfriend / husband / bodyguard is my source of protection.*

Fact #6: Oh, if only all of you readers had boyfriends or husbands the size of Vin Diesel, with the dexterity of Oscar De La Hoya, and the unmatchable strength of Hossein Rezazadeh (2004 Olympic gold-medal winner, also known as the world's strongest man). And oh, if only they were beside you twenty-four hours a day, seven days a week. Is this true for any of you reading this book?

This is a horrible myth and excuse for not educating yourself in self-defense. You'd think, especially in this day and age, that women wouldn't even have the nerve to verbalize this thought. But it's true; I hear them say it all the time in my workshops and through my general associations with women. This is nothing short of hogwash!

We live in an age where many women are stronger, better educated, more independent, and more self-sufficient than they would have been twenty or more years ago. Women are generally fervent in their demands for equality between the sexes. They want the same pay, the same respect, and the same opportunities men have. And I strongly believe women should get these things! However, why spend so much time and effort creating a melting pot of equal wants and needs when you wouldn't even consider spending an hour or two a week in learning how to protect yourself? It doesn't add up!

On a personal note, I'm all for chivalry, and I've got a beautiful wife whom I'd defend in a heartbeat. But I'm also not an idiot. I know I'm not with her twenty-four hours a day. And I'm aware that there are bad people around who, given the opportunity, would attack, harass, assault, or rob her. Because of this, she has become educated in self-defense.

Finally, this myth only takes the responsibility of self-protection away from you and places it into someone else's hands. It's a cheap excuse, and I'll go so far to say it's incredibly stupid. When you're standing eye-to-eye with a criminal who wants to assault you, show him the few tricks you have hiding under your sleeve instead of screaming for your boyfriend, husband, or bodyguard. In the words of Susan B. Anthony, "I declare to you that a woman must not depend upon the protection of man, but must be taught to protect herself, and there I take my stand."

Myth #7: *I'm too little. I'm too weak. I'm too small. My attacker will be twice my size and physically impossible to fight!*

Fact #7: On the surface, physical strength and size definitely appear to be the only factors in determining, say, the winner of a fight. Pair a five-foot-tall, one-hundred-pound man against a six-foot, two-hundred-pound opponent in a boxing match, and only the friends of the little guy would bet on him to win. We take a look at a tall, mean-looking man with bulging biceps and broad shoulders and we are automatically intimidated by his size and seeming strength.

However, winning doesn't directly relate to size or strength; it's in how you use your knowledge to your advantage. In self-defense, we are fighting an attacker's weaknesses, not his strengths. Self-defense is not a sparring match, it's using your mind to determine vulnerability and to consequently strike defensively. There are target areas on a human body that are extremely vulnerable. The effectiveness of your own physical strength lies in the power of your mind to use it correctly and strategically to your advantage. Chapter 4 details, at greater length, the power of the mind over muscle. Part II of this book will teach you where the physical vulnerabilities lie on a person.

Myth #8: *Who needs self-defense? That is what the police are for!*

Fact #8: In 1993, Daryl Gates, chief of the Los Angeles Police Department, stated, "There are going to be situations where people are going to go without assistance. That's just the facts of life." Ouch, the truth hurts, doesn't it?

Now, before any of you law enforcement officers, friends, or relatives start huffing and puffing in anger toward me and stop reading this book, please understand that I commend, respect, have confidence in, and support our local police officers. While they are the true heroes in each of our communities, they are not magicians. If you are in a threatening situation and instinctively respond by dialing 911 on your mobile phone, what happens next? You wait for the police to come. There is no magic formula to eradicate the waiting period; it's inevitable.

FAST FACTS

National response times for police assisting victims:

- Within five minutes   29.6%
- Within six to ten minutes   26.9%
- Within eleven minutes to one hour   33.0%
- Within one day   5.0%
- Longer than a day   0.1%
- Length of time not known   5.3%
- Not ascertained   0.1%

National Crime Victimization Survey
(Washington, DC: Bureau of Justice Statistics, 2002)

It's a little scary that most of the responses take a minimum of eleven minutes. I'm not suggesting that you become a vigilante and forget about dialing 911, but you need to be aware that during the time you wait for someone to arrive to aid you in a threatening situation, you can be severely injured or killed by a criminal. It makes sense to know how to protect yourself at whatever cost while you wait for help to arrive. You deserve and need that chance.

Myth #9: *I just can't do it! I'm not a fighter and can't imagine poking someone's eye out!*

Fact #9: It's silly, useless, and detrimental to accept victimization. The starting point of self-defense is to believe in yourself. When you have a high degree of self-esteem and self-confidence, you do not quietly welcome intimidation.

In 1993, Jeffrey Snyder authored an article for *The Public Interest* titled "A Nation of Cowards." In this piece, he marvels at the way popular culture strongly encourages an individual's right to self-expression and self-esteem, and wonders why society does not place even a minimal emphasis on self-defense. Snyder writes,

> . . . the media and law enforcement establishment continually advise us that, when confronted with the threat of lethal violence, we should not resist, but simply give the attacker what he wants . . . how can a person who values himself so highly calmly accept the indignity of criminal assault?

When you start to believe that your life and the lives of those you love are worth living and enjoying, you will do whatever it takes to survive and conquer a threatening situation. By doing so, you immediately give yourself permission to fight back. You will fight even though you're a lover. You will strike someone in the eye even if it grosses you out. You will scream, punch, kick, bite, scratch, and do whatever is necessary to get out of there alive. Because you are worth it!

If you continue to feed the mentality of *I can't do it*, you won't be able to do it. Having this type of negative attitude does a number of things. The most important is that it gives the criminal the upper hand. It puts you into an automatic position of defeat and turns you into another statistic.

True, using whatever physical force is necessary to promote survival doesn't paint a pretty picture. But neither does suffering from the mental and physical injuries from rape or spending three weeks hooked up to IVs after being beaten to a bloody pulp. Or being dead. It's your choice.

Myth #10: *I'll be so scared, it will paralyze me from taking defensive action. My fear will make self-defense impossible.*

Fact #10: Fear is *normal*. Whoever thinks that fear—to a small or large degree—should *not* be experienced as a reaction to a threatening or intimidating situation is foolish or naive.

Fear is natural. Fear is expected. But fear doesn't have to be a paralyzing mechanism that prevents a beneficial reaction. You need to decide what frightens you more—being dominated, injured, or killed by a criminal, or taking a risk and fighting back. Yes, you may hurt yourself somehow by protecting yourself against your attacker. His knife might nick your ear, a bullet from his gun may graze your head, and so on. But using self-defense is a means for escape and ultimate survival. If you're too scared to react defensively and opt instead to remain under an attacker's control, he'll have his way with you anyway. Chapter 4 will discuss turning fear into effective reaction.

If you have truly grasped the facts in this chapter, you probably want to know more. What is the next step? What more do you need to learn?

Awareness is one of the key pieces to this puzzle. The best form of self-defense is the kind you don't need to use. In other words, if you can avoid a potentially threatening situation, your best bet is to do so. The next chapter discusses important elements in assessing a situation to determine whether self-defense would be useful, necessary, or a waste of your time.

3

Pay Attention!
It Just Might Save Your Life

An ounce of prevention is worth a pound of cure.

—BENJAMIN FRANKLIN

The one guarantee we have in this life is that there are no guarantees. While self-defense is the best option you have to protect yourself when you are attacked, it doesn't promise that you will walk away unscathed— or even walk away at all. It would be absurd of me to tell you it works 100 percent, all the time. However, as shown in the previous chapter, statistically speaking self-defense is your best option if you find yourself in a physically compromising situation.

On the same note, being educated in self-defense does not grant you the right to play hero or God purely because you think you have the mental and physical capabilities to do so. First and foremost, common sense and good judgment need to be used—they might keep you from getting into an unfortunate situation. One of the first things I tell my workshop students is, "Come into my class, but park your egos at the door. If you choose not to do so, you don't belong in my class." It's mostly men who have a tough time hearing this statement. They are more apt to provoke altercations or position themselves in threatening situations rather than avoiding them. This is what I call the "curse of the tough man." There have been too many situations where I've seen a man, upon feeling slightly threatened, either generate tension to start a fight or immediately start pushing and shoving instead of walking away. Some men, if they feel someone is simply looking at them in a hostile or otherwise threatening manner, will aggressively confront the situation directly by using physical or verbal threats and even immediate physical action. They feel the need to use their testosterone in defense of their masculinity rather than good common sense by de-escalating what might turn into a dangerous situation. A lot of men think they can physically handle themselves against any other man, and therefore do not put much stock in developing awareness. They will not think twice about jogging late at night or parking their car in unpopulated and dimly lit areas. They are big, they are tough, and they can handle themselves.

However, the best form of self-defense is the kind you don't need to use. Using common sense and awareness creates preventive self-defense, which allows you to avoid potentially dangerous situations. It's ridiculous to purposely put yourself in a possibly hostile environment because you think:

- You can mentally or physically handle someone's bad or aggressive behavior.
- Nothing bad would ever happen to you.
- The threat seems manageable and there is no potential for escalation.

I've met too many people who dream of having a heroic story to share of how they have defended themselves against a thug twice their size. It's these same people who choose to use self-defense for all the wrong reasons, specifically pride, ego, or arrogance.

The first rule in learning self-defense is to understand what it means—defending against a viable threat when no other options conceivably exist. You only use it if you have to. In this chapter, you will learn:

- What potential existing threats are.
- What you need to pay close attention to.
- How to avoid becoming a possible victim.
- What makes you a potential target.

Where Are You? Location Matters!

Location is one of the most significant factors that prompt a criminal to decide whether or not he will carry out his crime. Generally speaking, criminal attacks do not occur in well-lit and populated areas. This type of environment does not promote convenience, accessibility, and a low (or no) risk of getting caught—the three elements that make a crime easy to execute. While it is infeasible that you will be able to control each environment you happen to occupy, there are certain places within your direct

---

FAST FACTS

About one in four violent crimes in 2003 occurred in or near the victim's home:

- About half occurred within a mile of home.
- Seventy-six percent occurred within five miles of home.
- Only 4 percent of victims of violent crime reported that the crime took place more than fifty miles from their home.
- Among common locales for violent crimes, other than the victim's home, were on streets other than those near the victim's home (17 percent), at school (14 percent), or at a commercial establishment (7 percent).

National Crime Victimization Survey
(Washington, DC: Bureau of Justice Statistics, 2003)

power where you can create the safest haven possible, especially your home and your car.

Home

People normally assume they are safe within the walls of their home, but this is not always the case. According to the 2003 *National Crime Victimization Survey*, twenty-nine out of one thousand homes were burglarized in 2003. So while being locked indoors is presumably safer than being outdoors, you are not completely inaccessible to criminals. In 2003, the FBI reported that *only* 62 percent of homes broken into required forcible entry. Burglars tend to look for convenience . . . an easy in and an easy out. The average criminal will spend, at most, approximately four minutes trying to break into a house. Anything that takes longer than that will discourage him, and he'll move on to his next attempt elsewhere. Again, convenience is the main issue. An open door, window, or garage is basically highlighting that a particular house is an open house. *Everyone is welcome, please do come on in.*

Below are some recommendations on what you can do to lower your chances of being victimized in your home. Most of these will seem obvious to you, but you may not be utilizing these suggestions on a regular basis.

• **Know who your neighbors are.** When you are friendly with and have even a minimal relationship with your neighbors, they customarily look out for you. I'm sure you would do the same for them.

• **Before answering the door, ask who it is.** There are a lot of safety tips we reserve for and reiterate to our children. "Never answer the door when the doorbell rings," we remind them. "First ask who it is. If it's a stranger, don't let him in." As adults, however, we seem to forget that this tip applies to us as well. How many of us open the door immediately upon hearing a knock or the doorbell ring? How many of us ask who it is or look through the peephole to see if it is anyone we recognize? Just because folks want to come in, it doesn't mean you have to let them. If it is a stranger asking for charitable contributions, directions, or dropping off a package, you are under no obligation to answer the door. If you feel unsafe or suspicious, trust that feeling in your gut and don't answer. Better safe than sorry.

• **Close and lock your doors and windows.** Obvious? Sure, especially at night, right? But how many of us lock our doors during the day when we're home? Having unlocked doors or open windows is basically an invitation for a criminal to come right in.

• **Close your garage.** Obviously, if you're working in your garage or in your driveway, an open garage is a necessity. But when it's not in use, why leave it open? To mark your home as an open house? To give someone (whom you'd rather not) the chance to walk into your home?

• **Change your locks when necessary.** Remember Caryn's story in the beginning of this book? She was almost raped in her apartment by a man who had a key from a previous tenant. When you move into a new home, change the locks! If you are living in a controlled apartment community, be sure management sends someone over to change the locks *when you are present* to ensure they did their job. If you move into a home, hire a locksmith to change the keyways.

• **Get a secure dead bolt for the door.** Dead bolts are a must for any door that can be opened from the outside. A couple of things to keep in mind: First, buy a quality dead bolt; this is one household item that you don't want to scrimp on. When you purchase it at your local hardware store, ask the professionals for the strongest dead bolt that is of top quality. And second, be sure it has no less than a one-inch throw—the length of the throw is what makes a dead bolt strong, so the longer the better.

Also, if possible, get a professional to install it for you or make sure you know how to do it correctly. If not installed properly, the dead bolt will not be effective.

• **Leave lights on.** Now, I don't want your electric bill to fly through the roof, but illuminated areas are a quick and easy deterrent against criminals. Leave a kitchen, bathroom, porch, or garage light on during the night. A couple of extra bucks on your utility bill might have deterred a burglar.

• **Use light timers.** Light timers are especially useful if you are not going to be home for a long period of time. Automatic timers can control interior or exterior sections to turn off during daylight hours. A home that looks lived in has a better chance of not experiencing an intrusion than one that looks dark and unoccupied.

• **Don't hide your keys.** While it may be convenient to leave a spare key under a mat, plant, or rock outside your front door—especially if you forgot your house key—it is *not* safe. Doing this creates an obvious invitation for criminals to enter your home. Most people know the typical places spare keys are left, and criminals are no exception. They know that the first place to look, if they hope to get a break in breaking into a home (no pun intended), is underneath the doormat . . . or under a nearby rock.

• **Get an alarm system.** Most times, if a criminal sees a warning on a house detailing that an alarm system is installed, he won't bother with it and will go to the next house. He doesn't want a challenging task; he doesn't want to get caught.

• **Change your routine.** This is universal defensive behavior that will detract a criminal who operates opportunely. A criminal who may be watching you for a period of time becomes accustomed to your activity and behavioral patterns. If he sees you leaving your kitchen light on at eleven o'clock each night, he knows this is nothing but routine behavior. If you leave it on from 8 PM, or switch on the living room light instead, this throws him off-guard. Remember, anything that can create confusion will make a criminal less confident of attacking you and lessens your chances of being victimized.

• **Place a blocking device, such as a piece of wood, in the track on sliding glass doors.** This is my mother's favorite. Once I moved away from home, the first thing she told me was to measure the track area on my deck door, go to Home Depot, have them cut a piece of wood that size, and place it in the track. Trust me, it works!

I know of a woman who, by using this safety tip, prevented an intruder from coming into her home. On a late Saturday evening, she and her brother were playing cards in the back room of the first floor of their house. A large sliding glass door, which almost extended to the full width of the back wall, stood only a foot or two away from them. As they continued playing, they heard footsteps outside the house right near the sliding door. In a matter of seconds, someone had started furiously pulling at the outside handle of the door, but the door wouldn't budge open because a piece of wood had been placed in the track area. My friend and her brother started screaming and threatened to call the cops as they started to dial 911. This person continued to violently pull the door handle back and forth, making so much noise that the door seemed ready to come off its track. Thanks to the blocking device, the door remained closed and locked. The person gave up and ran away.

Automobile

As with your home, being in or near your car is not always safe. Here are some rules to follow to increase your level of safety:

• **Park in lit areas.** I know that sometimes this is not possible, especially if you reside in a large, overcrowded city and parking garages are the norm. Still, try to choose spots that are filled with people and open places of business. Stay away from areas that make you intuitively uncomfortable. Trust your gut; you know when an area is sketchy.

• **Hide your valuables.** Don't draw unwanted attention by leaving your Rolex—okay, okay, your Timex—in plain view on the passenger seat. Hide your newly purchased items in the trunk of the car rather than in the front or backseat of your vehicle. Even leaving your mobile phone out may attract the wrong kind of attention.

• **Lock your doors.** Do so immediately when stepping into your vehicle. If you have young children, I know you do this as soon as your child is nestled safety inside the car. If you're quick enough to incorporate preventive measures to prevent your child unlocking your door at the most inconvenient time, use the same caution to prevent a stranger from having easy access to your vehicle.

• **When stopped at a red light, stay at least one and a half car lengths behind the vehicle in front of you.** Another one of my mother's favorite recommendations. This offers you a quick and easy escape should the need arise.

• **Look before you get in.** Before you get into your car, look underneath and inside it. You never know what you might find!

• **Pay attention to what and who is parked around you.** Unmarked vans are the number one type of vehicle that you need to be aware of. The vans I am referring to are not the modern-day SUV-type vehicles or minivans. Remember the popular vans during the 1970s? They were somewhat large, with a few windows, usually located on the back of the van and on the front doors. These vans look like they are used for construction or painting purposes, but they lack any verbiage indicating a particular company or crew. Generally speaking, they look out of place in a parking lot with other vehicles.

These unmarked vans block the view around your car because of their size. Also, they are ideal for use in criminal attacks because of the ease of entering and exiting. If you feel funny about seeing an unmarked van near your car that you didn't notice before, don't be afraid to look inside its windows. In the worst-case scenario, if there is a criminal inside who is waiting for the right moment to grab you, you might have surprised him instead.

Out and About

Your home and your car are the two places within your immediate control. You have the upper hand in choosing how you maintain a reasonable level of safety. But what about when you're jogging outside? Or taking a walk in a local park? What are some red flags and recommendations to heed within environments shared by strangers and not within your direct control? Below are some common examples of places and activities you might find yourself in and my correlating suggestions to heighten your level of awareness. The key in determining your safety level depends on what your common sense and your gut is telling you. You need to start listening. The majority of this advice is more applicable during evening hours, in venues that are dark and devoid of people.

  • **Jogging at night.** Don't do it if you don't have to. Burning extra calories or fashioning better calf muscles is not worth the possibility of being mugged, jumped, or raped. If you had a fourteen-year-old daughter who told you, at nine o'clock at night, that she was going outside for a run, I bet you anything you'd turn her right around and say, "Over my dead body!" Exert this same protective behavior for yourself as well as your loved ones. If you find yourself outdoors alone at night out of dire necessity, pay attention. Look around as you walk. Instead of staring straight ahead the entire time, turn around and see what is going on behind you. Or turn to the side periodically. Make sure that you have full vision of your environment.

• **Leaving places of business.** If you can find someone to walk out of the gym, your office, or a store with you, then do it. If you are uncomfortable walking to your car alone, don't do it. Find someone you can trust, call someone—do whatever it takes to make you comfortable. Being safe is all about being smart and feeling secure. If you have an opportunity to ease an unsettling feeling, use it.

• **At the ATM.** If you have to get out of your car to get to a machine, don't leave the car running or your doors unlocked while you get your cash. You cannot physically see your surroundings while your head is facing the machine, so anyone can hop in your car. Prior to using an ATM, take a good look around and assess your location. Is there anyone around who makes you feel nervous or anxious? Make your transactions as quickly as possible. Don't loiter, and don't spend any more time than you have to, especially at night.

• **At a nightclub or bar.** If you are at a bar or a nightclub, use caution. If you are a woman, know that there are some men who may be on the prowl, and you just might be in their path. Be leery of the guys who seem overly aggressive. Be particularly watchful if you are alone, and don't be afraid or embarrassed to enlist the aid of a bouncer. If someone is bothering you or making you uncomfortable, tell the bouncer. He is getting paid to maintain a safe environment for the venue's patrons. If no bouncer is present, tell a bartender or a manager of your situation. No one wants their place of business disrupted by disorderly conduct.

A Safety-Conscious Lifestyle

Crime is real. It's everywhere, in my neighborhood and in yours. And while we may resent having to arrange our daily routines in avoiding it, we need to find a balance between ignoring its existence and becoming its slave.

I'm sure you've heard these phrases many times: *Don't go out late . . . don't jog after eight o'clock at night . . . don't go anywhere by yourself.* Because we are warned that most criminal activity takes place at a certain time or place, these cautionary statements are sometimes used to instill fear in our minds. Additionally, they can be used to dictate how we should organize our lives and the activities we participate in. The trouble with this is that it can create an ineffectively high level of paranoia and indirectly bind us with a victim mentality. We give up our freedom and blindly follow a bunch of seemingly impossible rules to keep from becoming statistics. Should we be overwhelmed by fear and forfeit our leisurely activities because an attacker might lurk somewhere in a dark corner? Do we bolt our doors and windows and never leave the house? Do we become hermits because crime, in fact, exists?

Of course not—that's foolish. Giving up our natural rights in order to safely determine what we do and when we do it is one way of giving criminals the upper hand. On the flip side, this doesn't mean we should pump up our egos and act in a cockamamie manner to prove we will not be ruled by criminals. There is a fine line between developing common sense in determining our level of safety and doing whatever we want just because we have the innate liberty to do so.

And it is up to us to use proper judgment in deciding what that fine line is.

For example, why jog outside late at night when you can do it earlier in the day? Why walk alone in an isolated, sketchy area when your friend could have accompanied you? You need to understand that if there is something within an environment you can control or change, it is your responsibility to do so if it might prevent something bad from happening. If you feel uncomfortable walking to your car from the grocery store because there is an unmarked van parked next to your car, go back inside the store and ask someone to walk to the car with you. Again, use common sense.

Alone, Aware, and Able

Be aware of your surroundings sounds like such an elementary statement, you might not even bother with it. But remember, the best opportunity a criminal has to follow through with his attack on you is when you're oblivious to what's going on around you. His upper hand is the surprise tactic, striking you without warning. He will wait for you to be distracted by something—a crying baby, trying to find a ringing cell phone in your purse, or being mentally lost in your own world of personal thoughts. Once he has targeted you as being inattentive, he has more leeway to successfully attack you.

Being aware of your environment, your surroundings, and how you act and are perceived will make you significantly less vulnerable in many situations. The combination of what is happening around you and what you are or are not paying attention to is primarily what dictates whether or not a criminal will choose you as his target.

An attacker needs convenience, an easy in and an easy out. He ordinarily will not walk into a crowded park at noon and grab a woman to rape. He will wait until it's dark and there is no one around. He will wait for her to be afraid and to be intuitively uncomfortable. He knows this type of environment will make her nervous, afraid, and unconscious to any possible defensive opportunity because of her fear. Ordinarily, a person will not confront that eerie feeling of fear, but will ignore it and continue on as if nothing is wrong. If you find yourself in an environment that makes you uncomfortable, leave. Or, if possible, move toward a populated area. That is one thing, in itself, that will catch a criminal off-guard. He may even cross you off his list as a target.

My wife was a cheerleader for a professional football team when I first met her. Late one evening, she was leaving the football stadium to go home. When she got into her car in the parking lot, she looked at the gas gauge and realized she was almost out of gas. She drove to the nearest gas station, but it happened to be in a bad section of town near the stadium. She called me, and from the tone in her voice, I could tell she was worried.

"Do you really need gas?" I asked her. Now I was the one who was worried.

As it turned out, she had enough to get home. I managed to convince her to leave the station immediately and fill up her tank the next day. I'm always reminded of this situation when talking to people about the importance of self-safety. I suppose, when things get personal and you start to mull over possible bad things happening to people you love, your common sense starts to gain clarity.

I like to ask my students who have younger loved ones, especially children, whether or not they would encourage their kids to follow in their footsteps when it comes to safety awareness and action. Some of the foolish things adults do in comparison to younger people seem more socially acceptable, even if they break most safety rules. A good rule of thumb to use when assessing a situation is to think of your actions and whether or not you would suggest that someone you love copy them. If you're in a particular area that causes you distress, turn around and go home. It's what you would tell your child to do. Be smart about being aware.

We are responsible for gauging our intuitive level of comfort and using whatever resources we have around us to figure out how we can avoid a potentially bad situation. When in a group of two or more, your threat level is lessened; that's a fact. Being in or finding an environment where many people are around is critical. It is rare that a criminal strikes two or more people at the same time. The common criminals and the threats that worry us—rape, muggings, abductions—usually befall a sole individual in an isolated area. I understand that it is not always possible to be around a group of people, and I am certainly not discouraging you from going about your daily routine alone. However, if you find yourself in the middle of a threatening situation and you have an opportunity to move toward a crowd or a populated location, do it. No crook wants to draw attention to himself, so you can find yourself weakening what he thought was his greatest strength.

Some time ago, a friend of mine, Amy, was traveling in the left lane on a two-lane highway about five miles above the speed limit. There was a car behind her, tailing her in a dangerous and exaggerated fashion and swerving slightly from side to side. When she looked in her rearview mirror, Amy noticed that the driver seemed agitated and annoyed. Amy signaled and switched into the right lane. All she wanted to do was to get away from this crazy driver.

What happened? The other driver followed her over into the right lane and continued to tail her. My friend began to get concerned. Why was this driver intent on following her car so closely? Did she know this person? Was this a cruel prank? She had done nothing to provoke the agitation the other driver was clearly experiencing. Amy continued to switch lanes to prevent the other car from continuing to follow her. Similarly, the car continued to switch lanes to maintain a perilously close distance to her car. Amy became more frightened.

A couple of hundred yards away on the right side of the highway, there was a cemetery. Amy could see the tail end of a funeral procession moving toward the cemetery's entrance. She had found her opportunity to throw the enraged driver off-guard. As the erratic driver continued to tailgate her, Amy put on her right signal light and proceeded to enter the cemetery, following the funeral procession. The other driver followed her into the cemetery. Amy didn't blink. She switched her high beams on and drove deeper into the cemetery, blending in with the other cars as much as possible. About a minute later, the other driver made a sharp U-turn and peeled away, leaving only the piercing echoes of screeching tires behind. In her rearview mirror, Amy watched as the crazed driver disappeared, breathing a long-overdue sigh of relief. She found an opportunity to escape a potentially hazardous situation and she took it, rather than being paralyzed by fear and uncertainty.

Recognize the opportunities you have to avoid a bad situation and seize them. Put yourself in a populated area if possible and throw a bad guy off. Chances are, he won't follow your lead. Look around and pay attention. Criminals target persons who are oblivious, distracted, and unaware.

Your Gut . . . Trust Me, It's a Good Thing

Say you're walking down the street of a big city at seven thirty at night on your way to a friend's house for dinner. It's getting dark faster than you expected, and though you're following the handwritten directions your friend gave you, you're not exactly sure where you are. Walking swiftly, you pass Second Avenue . . . Third Avenue . . . Fourth Avenue. All of a sudden, your eyes are drawn away from the directions in your hand and you look around in annoyance, realizing you are completely and utterly lost.

You start to panic. *Breathe*, you tell yourself. *Breathe*. You look around and feel completely vulnerable because (1) you don't know where you are; (2) your mind is focused on figuring out where you might be; and (3) you are immediately limiting your self-protection because you are distracted. As you start to move forward toward the next block, you see two men propped up against the side of a building. You wonder if you should ask them for some directions and start walking toward their general locale. Three hundred feet away from where they stand, you start to feel uncomfortable and anxious. You get a deep sickening feeling in the pit of your stomach.

Something is telling you to turn around and head in the opposite direction. The warning voice in your head refuses to go away and only gets louder, matching the booming pace of your heartbeat. You pause, and that slight hesitation in your footsteps grabs the attention of those two men. Do you ignore your sixth sense and brush off your strange feeling as paranoia? Or do you take heed of the warning signals going off in your brain and run?

Intuition. All human beings, women especially, are blessed with this sixth sense. The failure to cultivate this inner knowledge and put it into practice on a regular basis is the fastest way for this inborn gift to lie dormant and ultimately useless. Using intuition can be as simple as spending a few minutes out of your day by yourself, connecting on a mental and spiritual level. It's about being aware of who you are, of where you are, and of others around you.

We often don't hone or respect our instincts because we don't want to become paranoid and make irrational decisions as a result. True, while we need to be able to trust our gut, our brains need to be equally involved in that process. Be smart. The best way to determine the usefulness and accuracy of intuition is to use it. And frankly, when it comes to deciding whether or not to confront a possible dangerous situation, if you begin to get that weak, sick, warning feeling, it's best to trust those cautionary signals and walk away. I'd rather err on the side of intuition than risk putting myself in danger. Wouldn't you?

What Do You Look Like?

No, I'm not asking for a physical description, but rather, how do you carry yourself? What does your posture look like? Do you slump your shoulders? When you walk, do your eyes follow your moving feet instead of looking straight ahead or around the area?

Studies have shown that communication between two people consists less of the actual verbal exchange and more of the way a person's body communicates.

- Seven percent of a conversation is represented by verbiage.
- Thirty-eight percent of a conversation is represented by the tone, volume, and pitch of the voice.
- Fifty-five percent of a conversation is represented by facial expressions and body posture.

Body language can do one of two things for you. It can help you avoid becoming a criminal's next target, or it can whet his appetite and make you his next victim. While I am not recommending you change a part of your personality, I am suggesting that how you present yourself to certain people is exactly what they use to try to figure you out. From a criminal's perspective, he will use your body language to see if you are quick prey.

I'm not trying to make you paranoid or nervous in thinking if you happen to be emotionally distraught and walking in a park at the same time, you are likely to be jumped, mugged, or raped. However, body language is another tool that can be used to heighten your level of awareness, measure your safety zone, and define the type of target you can be to criminals.

It can be difficult to interpret your body language on your own, so here is an opportunity to solicit the help of your friends and family. People who know you very well usually have a clear, unbiased image of how you present yourself. An assistant pastor I knew many years ago looked like he had a permanent scowl on his face and, therefore, gave the appearance that he was always either annoyed or in a bad mood. When one of his close friends mentioned this to him, the pastor was shocked! As it turned out, he had inherited his mother's mouth—the inner corners of his lips were naturally turned slightly downward, thus seeming to give him a permanent frown if he wasn't smiling. After hearing this comment, this pastor made a commitment to smile more and consciously turn his mouth upward, even if he wasn't grinning. As a result, he automatically appeared more approachable and less intimidating.

Our demeanor is typically unconscious, and being aware of how we present ourselves helps us to come across in a better light. What do your body language and general demeanor say to people? Below is a list of positive and negative images we may be projecting. Ask a friend or family member to circle the adjectives that describe you on a regular basis. While our body language and appearance may fluctuate with our moods, we do have standard dispositions during most of the time.

POSITIVE

- **Confident.** Do you have good posture? Are your shoulders back, chest out, stomach in, and back straight? Do you walk with a purpose—as if you have a clear destination in mind (even if you don't)? Having a confident attitude speaks volumes.
- **Self-assured.** Do you smile regularly and hold your head up high? Do you have a knowing look on your face, not one of confusion or doubt?
- **Aware.** Are you constantly looking around at your surroundings, noticing where you are and what is going on around you? Criminals don't generally prey on people who are paying attention.

NEGATIVE

- **Afraid.** Do you look worried or scared? Do you look as though you are lost and have no idea where to get where you want to go?
- **Distracted or inattentive.** Do you look as though you are living inside your own little world, oblivious to your surroundings? Even as simple a thing as bumping into someone accidentally is indicative of being inundated with distracting thoughts.
- **Under the influence.** Are your eyes bloodshot and droopy? Is your speech slurred, body posture sloppy, and do you seem generally out of it?

- **Insecure.** Are your arms crossed when you walk, as if you are really cold? Are your eyes focused everywhere except straight ahead?

Try this exercise. Whenever you are out and about on your daily routine, practice positive body language. Focus on maintaining good posture and being aware of your environment for a few weeks. If friends or family members noticed negative body language when you asked them about your projected image, see if they can notice a difference.

To Confront or Not to Confront— That Is the Question

Strong, confident people aren't afraid to confront a situation that is making them uncomfortable. In general, women tend to have a more difficult time with confrontation than men do. Many women avoid confrontation and offensive behavior, citing the following reasons:

- Offensive behavior goes against society's stereotypical depiction of the female nature—passive, quiet, and demure.
- They are afraid they will come across as being paranoid, bitchy, or aggressive.
- Confrontation will make matters worse and lead toward disaster.
- The other person will think of them in a negative light.
- They feel sorry for the other person and don't want to hurt anyone's feelings.

Having a strong knowledge that aggressive behavior is okay does not mean you have to confront every person with a highly offensive and high-strung attitude. It means you are not afraid to address a situation you don't feel right about. Most times, you can do this in a nonthreatening manner by making the other person aware that you believe your personal space is being invaded, and you are not happy about it. Most times the person will back off when confronted.

Here's an example. My friend Doris was at the grocery store with her sister checking out groceries in a self-checkout lane. They were taking an unusually long period of time doing this because most of their items required looking up bar codes. Luckily, there were five other lanes open and available so they wouldn't be holding up any other people behind them. A man got behind them and stood extremely close to my two friends. He was standing in such proximity that Doris could smell his breath and strong cologne. His presence was making her highly uncomfortable, especially in light of other available lanes he could have used. When my friend moved to the charge machine to swipe her debit card, he wouldn't budge to the slightest degree to allow her private access, but stood still. Doris was fuming at this point. She abruptly turned on her heel and faced him. Using a loud, strong voice, she said, "Excuse me, sir, you're in my way." He nodded and took a few steps back. Why he was standing so close and didn't even mumble a reply or apology, we don't know. But it doesn't matter. My friend confronted the situation in a powerful way without being violent, arrogant, aggressive, or threatening. And he did step back.

There are people out there who get off on intimidating others, particularly men who enjoy making women cringe in fear or feel awkward and inept. You need to stand up for yourself and not allow another person to invade your space and your comfort zone just because he wants to. And you don't need to remain quiet because you're afraid of hurting someone's feelings when it might turn out that he's really unaware of invading your space. Once again, it's better to confront a situation than be a sitting duck.

Being Present

One thing criminals don't want to see in a potential victim is a physical sense of awareness. They will typically not prey upon an individual walking down a street who appears to be looking around and mentally and visually absorbing her surroundings.

How many times have you walked down a sidewalk or in a shopping center and noticed absolutely nothing, because your sense of awareness was nonexistent? Given our active and engaged lifestyles, we probably wouldn't have noticed the color of the shirt we put on this morning if we weren't staring at it head-on in a full-length mirror.

I speak repeatedly about the lack of warning that precedes a criminal attack. It may seem that a guy spontaneously comes out of the clear blue and pounces on his unassuming and helpless victim, but you need to remember that he has probably been watching her for some time . . . noticing how the woman doesn't notice anything at all . . . watching how many times she has glanced at her watch in agitation. Next time you are walking somewhere, practice awareness. Notice how many people pass you. Are they mostly men or women? What are they wearing? Are they carrying shopping bags or duffel bags? Believe me, criminals notice awareness in people, and it's one thing that can prevent an attacker from deciding on you as his victim.

In Closing

There are different, suitable ways of responding to a situation, depending on its nature. Is someone unintentionally standing too close to you? Is he yelling at you at the top of his lungs for no reason? Is he acting agitated enough to physically attack you? There are definite factors to consider in determining what type of self-defense to utilize to de-escalate a potentially threatening situation. Here are some questions you want to ask yourself when wondering what you should do:

- **What kind of environment are you in?** Are you at home or in a strange area? Are you familiar with your surroundings? Are you at a park late at night or walking down a crowded street in broad daylight?
- **Are there people around?** Are there witnesses who could see the potential trouble that someone may be bringing your way? Can you enhance the general awareness of your total environment by loudly voicing your discomfort? Is there room for distracting or making a potential criminal feel uncomfortable?
- **Know the type of situation you are in and make appropriate provisions.** For example, if you are a woman and choose to go to a bar by yourself, know that guys will most likely be checking you out and hitting on you. Park close to the entrance of the bar, or valet your car if that is an option. Use the bouncer as the protective resource he is. Have him escort you to your car. If you go jogging in a park when the sun is setting, know that this situation makes you more vulnerable, and keep your eyes and ears open. As you run, use extra caution and pay attention.

4

Mind Over Muscle: What You Need to Know

The strong take from the weak,
but the smart take from the strong.

—UNKNOWN

Whether you're a golf fan or not, I'm sure you know Tiger Woods to be the top golf professional in the world. He's blown away doubly experienced peers and competitors while amazing his fans on a continual basis. Does he have raw talent alone? Or does his strong self-belief—his ability to think and decide he *will* win—have something to do with it?

In his book *How I Play Golf,* Tiger writes about the significant influence that both negative and positive thinking have over situations. He further explains that the power found in optimistic belief can ultimately pave the way toward victory and success. Tiger knows this is true; it happens almost every time he plays a match. In his game, when a win is at stake, he doesn't have room for doubts, negative thoughts, or the *I-can't-do-it* mentality. He doesn't have the luxury to doubt his abilities. He doesn't have the room to be defeated. And he doesn't have the margin to lose.

In a similar sense, self-defense is not about the sole use of your physical abilities or strength to dominate someone twice your size. The top concern I hear from women regarding their ability to use self-defense is their small size and lack of physical strength when compared with those of even an average man. While this concern doesn't necessarily stop women from wanting to learn self-defense, it can dampen their positive mental state by creating a sense of doubt. If you are resolute in accomplishing a goal this year, such as finishing your college degree or starting your own business or even writing a book, any doubt that comes between you and the desired achievement serves to lessen your overall level of confidence and can impede progress. Now, this doesn't mean you won't reach your goal; nor does it mean you don't believe in yourself enough. But the fears are distractions that keep you from making steady and consistent headway to ultimately reach your goal. They can rob you of your energy and your time.

It is not necessarily bulk or brawn that will ultimately save your life if you are being attacked. It is your mind, the greatest weapon of all, that allows you to focus on an attacker's weaknesses and not his strengths. This chapter concentrates on understanding the power of mental strength, which is ultimately greater and more effective than sole physical strength. Unlike lugging around a gun or knife or pepper spray, you don't need to make special provisions for battling criminals with your mind; it's with you at all times. You don't have to reach for it, and you don't have to look for it at the right time. It's right there with you, and in order to use it effectively and beneficially, you need to understand the four general rules in mentally preparing yourself for self-defense:

- Give yourself permission to fight back.
- Believe that you can physically fight back.
- Control fear; don't allow it to control you.
- Turn panic into reaction.

Think Positive

I have a friend who was determined to run a marathon in Alaska one year. Although she was about thirty pounds overweight, nothing could stop her from her desire to run twenty-six miles . . . not work, lack of time, energy, or even lack of physical ability. A month before the race, she realized her training in preparation for the marathon was, at best, inadequate. She didn't run every day, only a few times a week at most, and her longest runs did not exceed fifteen miles at once. A week before the race, her training hadn't improved in the least. The day of the marathon, she was afraid her lack of training would prevent her from finishing the race. She was wrong. During the entire twenty-six-mile run, she kept repeating over and over in her head, *You can do this. Just keep going. Run, walk, run, walk. Just don't stop. You can do this.* Needless to say, she completed her first marathon and attributed her success to that positive mind-set. "Without believing I could finish the marathon," she says, "I would never have done it, not even in a million years!"

Now, of course I don't approve of participating in strenuous physical activity without proper training, but my point is that her mind-set carried her through a difficult period of time. It works!

Let's talk about you. I'm sure you've heard many powerful stories about the concept of positive thinking and the multiple benefits created when we use mental strength to overcome physical obstacles that seem impossible. Reflecting back on your own life, what are some challenges that you have conquered through creating a positive mind-set in addition to believing and using the *I-can-do-it* mentality? In the space below, write down: (1) what those difficult moments were, (2) specifics as to the ideologies you formed to combat those difficulties; and (3) how you incorporated those ideologies into that time in your life to ultimately succeed.

How I Used a Positive Mind to Succeed

If You Don't Believe in Yourself, No One Will

Do you value your life? Do you value the lives of those you love, including your spouse, your children, or your parents? Do you care whether or not you live or die? Chances are all of your responses to these questions would be yes. Of course you care about yourself!

In my twenty-plus years of teaching self-defense, one of the biggest challenges I have faced, and still continue to encounter, is trying to help people realize the importance of self-esteem. The first step in learning self-defense is developing and maintaining self-confidence. If you don't believe in yourself and don't have even a slight amount of confidence, it is almost impossible to defend yourself. Why would you even want to save your life if it doesn't hold any worth in your own eyes? If that is the case, there is nothing worth fighting for. But I know you do care about yourself and love the people who are in your life. It's one of the reasons you picked up this book in the first place.

In *The Anatomy of Motive*, John Douglas (pioneer of modern behavior profiling for serial criminals and former chief of the FBI's Investigative

Support Unit) writes about his experience in how criminal predators target their victims. On a publicity radio tour, he remembers taking a call on a West Coast station from a woman whose daughter was acquainted with the convicted serial killer Glen Rogers. The woman asked Douglas what her daughter's chances were of being one of his victims, based on the mutual relationship they shared. Douglas asked her a series of questions relating to her daughter's personality characteristics. He asked if her daughter was an assertive and confident woman, to which the woman responded in the affirmative. So he told the woman that Rogers specifically chose targets who lacked self-esteem and were easily influenced. Her daughter's high self-confidence is what set her apart from his victims.

Recalling this conversation in his book, Douglas writes that one of the greatest weapons parents have against pedophiles is creating a solid sense of self-worth in their children. As we grow older, it is necessary to further develop and maintain this self-value, he explains, because adult sexual offenders are instinctually drawn to victims who have little to no self-confidence. They can almost pick their victims out of a crowd this way.

Please understand that this does not mean that any and all individuals with low self-esteem will automatically be targeted as victims and cannot employ self-defense tactics. Generally speaking, however, having an elevated self-value will increase your chances of survival. The basis of self-defense is in the value you place on yourself—your self-confidence. When you are aware of your worth and the impact you have on those around you, you can begin to understand the importance of protecting yourself.

You Have the Right to Protect Yourself; You Just Need to Take It

Give yourself permission to fight back. You might think that statement is absurd. You may feel that if you were the victim of a physical assault, there is no doubt that you would fight back, right? In my experience teaching self-defense, I have found the majority of women to be reluctant in learning and appreciating how to protect themselves.

Most of the people with whom I discuss self-defense, on both a professional and personal level, are hesitant in asserting an absolute commitment to following through with physical self-defense when appropriate. Whether this feeling stems from having a victim mentality or worrying about possible legalities, there is an overwhelming inner barricade that prevents many people, particularly women, from accepting their natural right to protect themselves. The first step in overcoming this obstacle is having a strong sense of believing your life is worth living, enjoying, and protecting.

The consequences of being a victim of a criminal act are horrible, and none of us in our right mind would choose to accept those consequences if given a chance, however slight, to prevent them. Let's imagine a legitimate fortune-teller existed. She proceeded to tell you that in one month, a man would break into your home late at night in an attempt to sexually assault you. While she couldn't guarantee the end result, she told you that if you fought back to the best of your ability, there would be an 80 percent chance you would successfully defy his advances and he would leave you untouched and unharmed. Would you have to take even twenty seconds to figure out what to do? Of course not. You'd make up your mind to fight back, to defend yourself against a person determined to destroy your life.

So why is it so hard for women to fully grasp the allowance they have been born with to self-protect? There are a variety of reasons. Throughout my many years teaching self-defense workshops, I have heard countless excuses to justify the disbelief in accepting self-defense as a necessity. They include:

- A criminal will not hurt me if I comply with his every demand.
- I will be accused of having provoked the criminal incident because

I was too aggressive and presumptuous in thinking I could protect myself.

- It won't help. I'm powerless. Self-defense is not an option.
- I don't think I can do what you're telling me to do. I can't do it.

Believing in these statements is the quickest and surest way to become a victim and stay a victim. I am astonished at how often I hear these excuses. It seems that these women believe it is easier to submit to the unlawful and barbarian domination of a criminal than to stand up and fight back. One of the ways to overcome these barriers is by recognizing that an attack is personal. Once realized, this statement opens up an area in your mind that provides the freedom for self-defense.

So what does giving yourself permission to fight back really mean? It means making a conscious decision, in this present moment, to accept the necessity and the execution of physical self-defense if you find yourself in a threatening situation. Remember, survival doesn't depend on excuses, it relies upon confidence and doing whatever it takes to make it out alive. If you don't start believing that you have permission to fight back, you will not be able to defend yourself should the need arise. If you don't give yourself this necessary permission, that's fine. You will just have to deal with a greater unknown and fear—being completely defenseless against a criminal. Without mental preparation and acceptance, there is no physical defense.

Read the affirmations below out loud with a strong and genuine belief. That faith is required to begin to learn and utilize proper self-defense.

- I believe in myself and in my matchless worth.
- I believe I have a duty to protect myself if I am in danger.
- I believe in standing up for my right to defend my life.
- I believe in carrying out physical self-defense to whatever extent in order to go home alive.

Never Predetermine Yourself to Be a Victim

Walking into a violent situation with a predetermined victim mentality—an inner sense of helplessness—will, most likely, mark your defeat even before you have a chance of defending yourself. This goes back to my firm belief in self-confidence being the bedrock for making self-defense work to your benefit.

How do you know if you have the victim mentality? Now, I understand that not every reader of this book will relate to having a victim mind-set, and that's wonderful! Or you may have only a slight degree of this mentality, but remember, the slightest sense of doubt can have a negative impact on learning self-defense. If you think any of the thoughts noted below, it is plausible that a portion of your mind may be geared toward seeing yourself as an automatic victim—even if nothing has happened to you! Use these guidelines to ensure that your level of confidence and strong positive attitude are maintained and developed.

THE VICTIM MENTALITY
- I can't do anything right, so why even try?
- If someone is out to get me, there is nothing I can do to stop it.
- Why bother?
- I am limited by my abilities.
- I can't. I can't. I can't.

Having this type of negative mind-set when you begin to learn about self-defense:

- Prevents you from believing in yourself.
- Enforces a false determination that you are physically unable to defend yourself.

- Gives immediate control to your attacker in determining the outcome of a situation.
- Transfers the responsibility in maintaining the welfare of your life from you to (1) chance; (2) fate; and (3) your attacker.
- Uses fear to overwhelm and ultimately paralyze a reasonable course of action that might save your life.

The bottom line? Having a victim mentality doesn't work. It doesn't help you out in any way, shape, or form. I am not advocating that you start believing you are a superhero—invulnerable, invincible, and untouchable by any and all human beings. I am suggesting you re-create your current mind-set, eliminating the unnecessary and harmful conclusions that say you are no match against an attacker. Instead of immediately affirming a plethora of false statements that form the basis of *I can't fight back*, start to visualize you as a victor instead of a victim. By living life with a victim mentality, you create defeat by merely breathing and living. Having a champion attitude creates positive thinking and continually builds strong confidence and, ultimately, success.

Fear: A Love–Hate Relationship

John is walking toward his apartment door one early evening after work. He carries a hefty laptop case under one arm, and is trying to maintain a strong grip on a bundle of mail with one hand while trying to fish his house key out of his deep trench coat pocket with the other. He is thinking, *Boy, I'm pooped. I hope I haven't missed the first part of* The Apprentice. *Where are my darn keys?*

Out of nowhere a tall, muscular man jumps out from the bushes, violently shoves John to the ground, and keeps him in place with his steel-toed construction boot. Though John is lying facedown on the pavement and has limited peripheral vision, he can see the outline of a gun that the stranger has pulled out of his jeans. The gun is aimed directly at John's head. In a brief second, John's life flashes before his eyes. Fear runs through every pore and vein in his body. He is sweating and his eyes are tearing up. Fear is paralyzing him, leaving him with no options for survival. Wouldn't *you* be frightened out of your mind?

Fear is the natural reaction our body exhibits when confronted with a threatening situation. It is a reaction that can make or break us depending on how we manipulate that response. Is being afraid a sign of weakness, powerlessness, or cowardice? Of course not, but there are some folks out there who believe and teach fear to be a completely useless and irrelevant emotion . . . claiming it is a feeling that can be easily switched on or off whenever we choose. This is nothing short of senseless machismo and stupidity. If some guy waves a large switchblade right in front of your eyes, you will not respond with apathy. You will be scared, and what you have to understand is that fear is normal. Fear isn't a terrible thing in and of itself; it is what you decide to do with it that determines a positive or negative outcome.

By definition, fear is a feeling of agitation and anxiety caused by the presence or imminence of danger. It can be used as an intuitive warning tool or as a paralyzing force. Fear can transform into a fierce, crippling emotion when you allow it to overwhelm you and control your actions to your sole disadvantage. The good news is that it doesn't have to.

GOOD FEAR
- Prompts you to take a proactive measure in making your life better.
- Acts as a survival mechanism, telling you when something is wrong.
- Motivates you to work harder, faster, or better.

BAD FEAR

- Paralyzes you and therefore prevents you from acting in your own best interest.
- Depletes your self-esteem and your ability to perform.
- Provokes irrational and illogical thoughts and actions.

Fortunately, there are ways to encourage good fear, and discourage bad fear.

Fight or Flight?

When we have been threatened and are in immediate danger, our mind and body automatically respond with fear. Fear of what? The most common fear generated from criminal attacks is of being injured by the criminal—being raped, battered, beaten, bruised, or killed. This fear is used to foster the victim mentality described earlier in this chapter and to eliminate all sense of the necessity for self-protection.

While fear is commonly related to an emotive reaction, there is more of a biological function at work than we may realize. This is commonly referred to as the "stress response" or the "fight or flight" mechanism. When we understand what physically happens to our bodies when stimulated by stressful situations, it becomes easier to understand how this can be used to our advantage for self-defense.

When you're faced with a threat, here is what happens in a matter of seconds:

- Your body begins to produce hormones (cortisol, epinephrine, and norephinephrine) that are being continuously pumped into your bloodstream.
- Your heart rate speeds up.

- Your blood pressure starts to rise.
- You start to sweat.
- Your pupils start to dilate.

Your brain is basically telling your body that something is wrong, and your body reacts in powering on its survival mode switch. The benefits of having this survival mode stimulated is that it does give you greater strength, faster speed, and a higher pain threshold until your body goes back to normal.

The problem is that this function takes place in a short period of time, within a few seconds, and if you don't make a decision—*run like the wind* or *fight to stay alive*—your body can get overstimulated and may very well freeze up. What your body is telling you is, *Hey, something is really wrong here and I'm providing you physical resources to do something about it. Now decide.* And you only have a few seconds, if you're lucky, to make up your mind.

Mental preparation is essential in learning how to properly defend yourself. By preparing your mind at this very moment, you can train your mind and body how to react in response to a future attack. The mental state you create and believe today is what will be triggered when you are forced to immediately react in response to a hostile situation. Should you refuse to believe what I am writing about in this book—the importance of believing in the freedom you have and the confidence you need to use self-defense—you will likely become too overwhelmed to react in a manner that will save your life.

The key is in forming your ideologies of self-defense, your methods of offensive and defensive behavior, so that when you are attacked, your mind will be reminded of those beliefs and act accordingly.

From Fear to Action

The number of self-defense or martial arts classes you may have taken means zilch when your mind has not been trained. If you haven't been educated in the importance of mental preparation, your jabs, punches, and kicks will do as much damage as trying to fend off an attacker with a Q-tip.

From the time we were small children, we have been taught to remain calm and not panic in life-threatening situations. If your house catches on fire, remain calm. If you find yourself caught in your vehicle after a devastating crash, don't panic. Hmm. This is a good theory, but difficult to practice. Fear is as real as a life-threatening situation, so when it's provoked, it's provoked. You can't prevent it from happening, but what you can do is to stop it from overwhelming you.

As I've stated before, your mind has to be made up well in advance of an attack as to what to do when your life is in danger. You need to know now that if you're attacked, you are going to fight back. If you don't know now, believe me, you will not know when you most need to know. It's this knowledge that can advantageously transform fear into anger and, ultimately, into physical defensive action.

Anger? Anger isn't a good thing, right? Isn't that what makes people hostile and turns them into monsters and maniacs? Not necessarily. The anger that I am referring to is a righteous, non-over-aggressive emotion. Raw anger stemming from motives of hate, revenge, and desired destruction is primarily a psychological issue. Righteous anger is what is created when your life, your being, your sense of self, and your family are on the brink of being snuffed out and you only have a brief period of time to act defensively.

This anger is stimulated when you remember in an attack that your child might be motherless if you succumb to a victim mentality. It comes when a complete stranger, who has no right at all, is putting his hands on you in attempt to abuse your sexual being. It comes when a criminal is doped up or blitzed out of his mind and has targeted you as his next prey just because he sees you.

While fear has a definite paralyzing mechanism, you need to understand and be convinced that it is not a continual force and, as a result, can be manipulated to your advantage. When you are in a situation where your life is at stake, you don't have the luxury of time to freak out. The time you have needs to be utilized to act, not react with an overbearing emotion. You cannot afford to waste moments crying and screaming; those moments need to be left for reactive defense. Cry and scream and freak out afterward.

Take a moment away from reading this book and start to meditate on the things in your life that are most important to you. What brings tears of joy to your eyes? What makes you laugh until your stomach begins to cramp up? Who makes you smile by remembering his face, or the way she smells, or how he makes you feel? What do you enjoy most in life? What do you want to accomplish in five years? Ten years? What do you live for? What do you work so hard on achieving? Now write them down in the spaces below.

The People, Dreams, and Things That Mean the Most to Me

_____

_____

_____

_____

_____

_____

_____

_____

_____

_____

Take another brief moment and read the list back to yourself out loud. Now imagine being raped or beaten or even murdered. In a matter of a few moments, all of the dreams, people, and plans you wrote about will be damaged or destroyed. The world you have written about will be shattered. You will never be the same again. Obviously, this will evoke some type of emotions in you. Sadness will probably be first.

Now think about being in a potential deadly situation where someone is clearly trying to violate you or take away your life. Tell yourself that there *is* something you can do about it. Being attacked doesn't mean you have to go home broken or in a body bag. Believe that you have the power to defend yourself and fight for your life. Tell yourself that you can survive.

More than likely, you will start to get angry and indignant. Let this anger fuel your drive to fight back. The key is thinking about it and be-lieving it now, not while an attacker has thrown his first punch. If you are attacked, you will be reminded of your beliefs, and the fighting and sur-vival instincts will be put to action. There is an old saying: "Chance favors the prepared mind." When your mind is prepared well before physical self-defense is necessary, you will be able to fight back without falling into the useless paralyzing power of fear.

Developing the Right Mind-Set

So how do you start to develop the type of mind-set that can be utilized to your benefit in the hour of need? Below are four principles that need to be practiced regularly, starting this instant. By practice, I mean intro-ducing a repetitive way of thinking. You can't practice confidence in the same way you can practice the piano, but you can remind yourself of your self-worth every day in order to increase your level of self-confidence.

- **Give yourself permission to fight back.** Understand that there is no one who has a right to harm you physically, emotionally, spiritually, or mentally. You do not have to be subject to a criminal's dangerous and reckless whim, and you can do something to avoid his lethal behavior. Believe that a criminal does not have the power to decide your fate, but you do have a responsibility to take control of situations when opportunities present themselves.

- **Renew your confidence.** Remember, you are worth it! Your life is worth having and maintaining. You are needed by your family and friends. You deserve to enjoy your life and fill it with laughter, peace, and love. Nobody has a right to take those priceless things away from you because he feels like it. Remind yourself that you are worth fighting for!

- **Take self-defense seriously.** Become educated and aware of the amount of violence that exists in today's culture. Don't tune out the media reports of criminal activity, or become numb to hearing about such attacks. Understand that crime exists, and that it is our responsibility to do our part in protecting our lives through awareness and through physical self-defense. Start believing that your chances of survival are greater if you fight back in order to promote an understanding that self-defense does work.

- **Visualize victorious situations.** We are often told to visualize our goals and dreams coming to fruition during the process of working toward them. In the same sense, visualize being attacked, mugged, or raped, and picture yourself using your mental knowledge and physical abilities to combat potentially deadly situations. Picture the criminal being so surprised by your defiant and defensive efforts to protect yourself that he balks and steps away from you. Picture him running away because you made a decision that he will *not* win.

Finally, remember that the time to start learning and practicing these behaviors is now. There is no greater time than the present. If you wait until you are in harm's way, it might be too late.

5

Behind the Faces of Crime

*We find that criminals know that what they are doing is wrong;
they know exactly that this is not the way that life should be played.
Therefore, they will always find the formula to make wrong right for them.*

—LYDIA SICHER

They kill, they brutalize, they rape, and they steal . . . among other things. Who are the bad guys whom we have often warned our children about? Who are the imprisoned criminals that stare at the world with lifeless eyes and a guiltless conscience? What motivates them to break the law and ruin the lives of innocent victims? Are they born or are they made?

When we were younger, it was easier to distinguish between a "good" and a "bad" person. The bad person was usually a stranger who tried to get us in his unmarked van with the lure of candy or kittens. A good person was predominantly defined as anyone well dressed, gentle-mannered, and somewhat unassuming. I think Ted Bundy pretty much ruined the assumed "good" stereotype.

For many years, professionals have attempted to delve into the criminal mind through extensive investigation, including criminal profiling, forensic analysis, and psychological research. The lay public is fascinated by this type of investigative work that aims to find out why heinous crimes are carried out. And the pros continue to scrutinize the criminal mind with sheer determination, fervor, and even obsession. Dr. James Alan Fox—the Lipman Family Professor of Criminal Justice, former dean at Northeastern University in Boston, and author of sixteen books—has said, "It is literally impossible to identify the few needles in a large haystack of people who fit the profile of a serial killer or mass murderer."

This chapter is included to provide a mini crash course on specific types of criminals so you can gain a better understanding of their methods of operation and their behavioral characteristics. They all have different motivations, addictive tendencies, family backgrounds, and personal experiences, so to reduce their psychology to a bullet-point list seems rather inadequate and, more important, practically impossible. There are wonderful books out there that discuss the mind of criminals in great detail, specifically those written by John Douglas, a leading expert on criminal personality profiling. While there are different levels of criminals, from those committing minor crimes such as pickpocketing to more serious criminals like murderers, this chapter will be focusing on those individuals who commit violent crimes and major crimes.

Don't Judge a Book by Its Cover

While unfortunate and basically ineffective, most people use their own personal method of criminal profiling. They read too many true-crime books and watch too many crime movies and documentaries—or not enough, for that matter—and base their judgments on the quality and quantity of information being downloaded into their brains. Some people establish these methodologies from their own personal experiences, prejudices, and opinions. So what can we do? And how can we tell if our next-door neighbor is the next Jeffrey Dahmer?

You need to realize that criminals come in all shapes and sizes. They are tall, short, fat, skinny, good looking, not so good looking, boisterous, egotistical, shy, quiet, sexual, asexual, multiply-tattooed, tattoo-free . . . you get the picture. The first key in understanding criminals is to understand that they can look like anyone. Here are some examples of a wide range of criminals and the crimes they've committed:

- In 1968, Mary Bell, a sweet-looking eleven-year-old English girl, was convicted of strangling two little kids to death.
- Edmund Kemper, a six-foot-nine giant, was convicted of killing eight women, one of whom was his mother.
- The "Ken and Barbie Killers," Paul Bernardo and his wife, Karla Homolka, were a handsome couple living in an affluent community who raped and killed three young girls from 1990 to 1992. One of the girls was Karla's sister.
- In 1995, an unassuming housewife, Susan Smith, killed her two little boys by strapping them into their car seats in the family vehicle and watching it roll down a ramp into a lake.

The Devil Made Me Do It

". . . they acted human. But they weren't. They began to howl things. They wanted to get at children, to tear them up." David Berkowitz, infamously known as the Son of Sam, claimed he heard voices coming from his neighbor's Labrador retriever. This prompted him to begin a thirteen-month killing spree.

It is easy to point an accusatory finger at an imagined evil deity that commands a helpless mind to commit acts of savagery. Doing this establishes a criminal as insane and automatically excuses that person from responsibility for his own actions. In a way, it also eases the minds of average people, like you and me, by creating a sort of algebraic formula for killers. Mentally insane + related lack of rational thinking = murderer. A + B = C.

Not all violent criminals are mentally incompetent, however; nor are they excused from society because of the absence of a moral conscience and understanding of right and wrong. People with varying forms of mental illness can tell the difference between right and wrong—although there are severe cases where the law determines a criminal to be insane and thus not accountable for irrational thinking and illegal actions.

Can mentally stable and relatively normal people commit murder or rape? What is going on in their heads? Why do thieves steal, rapists rape, and killers kill? Motivating factors that create and stimulate criminal activity vary from person to person, but there seems to be an underlying theme. Criminal expert John Douglas suggests that most criminals have a common denominator leading them to commit crimes: Their main goal in life is to manipulate, dominate, control.

Crimes aren't committed for the sake of being committed. Among a plethora of other reasons, criminal activity is used as a tool to act out aggression, to maintain control over an out-of-control life, or to give sexual or emotional release. For example (and I'm sure you've heard this before), rape is not about sex; it's about control, humiliation, and dominance. In Douglas's book *The Anatomy of Motive*, he writes that the main motivation of criminals is a desire for power and control stemming directly from past experiences where they felt weak and out of control. In a way, it's almost as if criminals are getting back at whatever they experienced or whoever tried to hurt them.

Other motivating factors include:

- Money or greed
- Power
- Sexual pleasure
- Political issues
- Revenge
- Pure thrill

Born or Made?

When many parents find the forbidden pack of cigarettes a teenage child kept hidden in the sock drawer, the color drains from their faces and their minds begin to churn: *Oh my God, first cigarettes, then marijuana, then cocaine, then prostitution, and then . . . oh my goodness!* Does this mean that any child who engages in illegal or delinquent activity will become a Ted Bundy one day? Of course not.

Nobody wakes up one day and decides, *Today is the day I begin my violent criminal career. Hmmm, who can I rape today?* In the majority of studies profiling violent criminals, there were clear warning signs during childhood of overly aggressive, peculiar, and violent behavior that accelerated throughout the years. For example, you may study an older mass murderer and see past experiences of domineering or bullying of younger siblings, instances of arson or petty burglary, and so on. As they get older, the crimes increase and become more serious.

There are specific factors of influence, namely abusive childhoods and backgrounds, that can create a breeding ground for seeds of bad behavior. Now, we all carry some form of emotional scars from growing up; some are dreadful, and others are manageable. Every individual is given a personal choice to determine the extent of influence a bad past has over a future. I have seen folks who were severely physically and mentally abused as children grow up to be well-adjusted adults determined to make a good life. On the flip side, I have seen people with similar backgrounds ultimately taking a turn for the worse, tumbling downward into addictive behaviors, abusive actions, and even criminal activity

It boils down to having a choice. Criminals are not born with bad blood, but do tend to have turbulent backgrounds that create tendencies toward violence. Most times, these tendencies are self-fed and progress into deeper and more violent behavior. Professionals are still wondering why and how some people turn out good and others turn out bad. Human behavior remains quite a mystery to even the most knowledgeable psychologists and experts. We're all trying to figure it out.

While we cannot control the behaviors and actions carried out by violent people, we should have a concrete awareness that they are out there. They exist to dominate, control, and manipulate the lives of innocent people. Knowing this should not create a sense of hopeless vulnerability or ineffective fear, but rather instill a desire to learn how we can protect ourselves should we encounter such folks. Again, while this book is not the answer in evading criminals completely, it will teach you ways of self-preservation.

What to Watch Out For

As mentioned above, there is no magic formula in determining whether or not a person has criminal tendencies based on appearance alone. Additionally, it can be almost impossible to pick a potential criminal out of a crowd based on a single encounter. There are, however, general behavioral patterns you can look out for that should trigger your awareness.

• **Does the person look out of place?** Is he wearing clothing, for example, that is not appropriate to the weather, venue, or activity? Most people will not wear trench coats and boots in balmy eighty-degree weather, or formal attire during an outdoor baseball game.

• **Is the person exhibiting overly aggressive and hostile behavior?** While any average human being will get frustrated and irritated from time to time, there are those with hostile temperaments who take things to the next level and, thus, present a cause for concern. Say you're at a restaurant and a woman in a party next to you starts complaining to her waitress about the bad service she believes she is experiencing. Most people will communicate their disappointment using a strong, firm tone indicating their dissatisfaction without projecting extreme and outright anger. If this woman starts throwing plates or silverware, yelling or screaming, or threatens or uses physical force, she has crossed the line and is displaying signs of dangerous behavior.

• **Is the person paying an inordinate amount of attention to you?** Beware of people who have developed an obsession with you. If you are barraged with constant stares for long periods of time, being sent unwelcome gifts on a regular basis, or feel that your personal physical space is being violated (someone who stands, talks, or walks right beside you or in your face), confront the situation. Each of the items may be innocent in and of itself, but when there are multiple warning signs happening simultaneously, you need to start using extra caution.

• **Does the person seem to be exhibiting signs of antisocial personality disorder (APD)?** Now, I understand that not every human being is blessed with a charming, outgoing, and friendly personality, and being a shy, reserved, or introverted person does not call for an official diagnosis of APD. I'm talking here about a distinct disorder that is common to most convicted criminals, according to statistics. Clinical symptoms include failure to conform to social norms, manipulative behavior, impulsivity, general apathetic temperament, disregard for personal safety or that of other people, and lack of remorse or guilt when appropriate.

• **Does a person exhibit excessive physically violent behavior?** Physical violence upon another human being and destruction of property are obvious signs of an underlying problem. This could mean anyone from a man who beats his wife, to a young woman who repeatedly kicks her pet, to a teenage arsonist. You also need to be aware of people who regularly use physical means to release negative emotions, such as punching a wall, throwing objects, or kicking car doors in a fit of rage. These people could also be obsessed with violence, such as regularly reading magazines, listening to music, or watching television shows and movies that have predominantly violent themes.

• **Do you get a nagging, bad feeling in your gut?** There are certain uneasy, nagging feelings that are created upon meeting someone or being in a certain situation. People usually think something like, *Well, something just doesn't feel right* or *There's just something strange about that guy, I don't know what it is.* Our bodies and minds are truly our personal bodyguards and tell us when something feels or is wrong. Gavin de Becker, a leading expert in violent behavior, wrote a marvelous book titled *The Gift of Fear,* which thoroughly examines the purpose and benefits of intuition. In this book, he offers several survival signals that our bodies give off to warn us of possible dangerous situations or people. They include persistent thoughts, wonder, anxiety, hunches, gut feelings, doubt, fear, apprehension, hesitation, and suspicion. If something doesn't sit well inside, it would serve to listen and heed the warning, rather than brush it off as paranoia.

Remember, just because someone exhibits strange demeanor or action, it doesn't mean you should report him to the police or respond by verbal accusations. It means you need to keep an open eye on the person and the situation you are in. Keep a low profile, but simultaneously remain sharp and observant to see if the behavior worsens.

What Criminals Look For

Just as we all have a responsibility to be aware of suspicious behavior in other people, we need to be aware of what criminals may be looking out for in their selection of victims. Could we unknowingly be at risk of being targeted? A word of caution needs to be expressed here. Victims may be chosen randomly or selectively, and broad definitions of what criminals look for need to be digested with a grain of salt. Ted Bundy targeted women with long, dark hair, similar to the girlfriend who had broken up with him years prior to the start of his killing campaign. Other criminals choose victims simply because they happen to be at the wrong place at the wrong time.

Most criminals don't want to get caught and so will choose victims with that premise in mind. For that reason, a criminal won't typically target people who are aware of their surroundings, who appear confident and self-assured, and who are in a populated setting, particularly during daylight hours. This is why I have stressed paying attention and avoiding being alone in dark places; it statistically lessens your chance of becoming a victim.

While victimology—the thorough study and analysis of victim characteristics—is an integral part of solving crime and profiling criminals after the fact, it is a challenge to pinpoint potential victims before a crime occurs. Brent Turvey, an expert in forensic science, defines victim potential in terms of general risk assessment, from low to high. What variables constitute an elevated risk for a person to experience a criminal attack? These can include many factors that revolve around lifestyle. For example, a person who regularly travels alone, abuses drugs or alcohol, and lives in a relatively high-crime area is at a high risk of becoming a victim of crime based on these factors. One who has a lot of friends and family, doesn't go out much, and pays attention to surroundings is at a low risk of becoming a victim. Below are a few factors that may increase the risk:

• **Emotionally unstable or volatile behavior (aggressiveness, emotional outbursts).** When you're emotionally charged, your sense of awareness is decreased. If you get into a fight with your spouse and leave the house in a state of frenzy, anger, or frustration, there is nothing on your mind other than the fight. You don't think about where to go, who is around you, or what you are doing. You are only thinking of how angry you are because of what your spouse did or didn't do. Not paying attention makes a person instantaneously vulnerable to criminal attacks.

• **Impulsivity.** While spontaneity can be a good thing, it is important to keep an eye on impulsive behavior. Do you participate in, without questioning, certain activities that may be harmful to you because you want to have fun or it feels good? How often do you weigh the consequences that may result from certain immediate decisions you make? If you are at a bar one evening with your friends and some guys try to convince you to go back to their place for an extravagant party, saying yes without rationally thinking about it may increase the risk of something terrible happening. It doesn't mean they are bad guys, necessarily, but it does mean the chances of being physically or sexually assaulted are more prevalent if you go than if you say no.

• **Choice of friends and social settings.** Whom do you hang out with and where do you generally spend your social time? Certain people and settings will expose you to violence and make you more susceptible to crime. Spending every night smoking weed in a deserted parking lot with your friends increases your chances of becoming a victim of crime. As adults, our friends and their lifestyles might seem like an obvious factor to consider in evaluating our lifestyles, but there is some behavior we excuse instead of paying more attention to. If your friends ask to you hang out in an area of town that makes you nervous or uncomfortable, you don't have to go. Why risk it?

• **Low self-esteem.** People who have no regard for themselves just don't care, period. They don't take the time to personally invest in their emotional, mental, spiritual, and physical well-being. As a result, they make pretty good targets. Why? They're not paying attention to what's happening around them. Chances are, they won't defend themselves against an attacker. And, their generally passive behavior makes them extremely vulnerable to encountering criminals and falling for their manipulative actions.

There are no black-and-white answers on who will become a victim. The most important things to consider are the lifestyle you maintain and the extent of your awareness. Doing so does lessen the risk of becoming attacked. I know of a woman who, when she was eighteen years old, took a trip to Tampa, Florida, with her older sister. They were drinking in a club when they met two good-looking young men who seemed charming and intelligent; they paid the girls a lot of complimentary attention. They said they were part of a bachelor party group being transported around town by a party bus. They asked the women to join them on the bus, and the women accepted. The next couple of hours were spent going from one bar and nightclub to the next. Luckily and thankfully, nothing bad happened. Nobody got raped, killed, or beaten. However, looking back at her experience, my friend is completely embarrassed that she and her sister accompanied a group of complete strangers on this moving party. She knows that both of them were at a high risk of being raped and is grateful that nothing bad happened. She doesn't do things like that anymore!

Take the time now to examine your life—past experiences, events, and encounters that may have increased your chance of becoming a victim of crime. Write them in the spaces below; it will help to increase your awareness of factors that may lead to an unsafe situation. It could be anything from accepting a ride from a stranger or passing acquaintance, to attending a social function that made you feel uncomfortable.

The Experiences That Might Have Heightened My Risk of Being a Victim of Crime

_____

_____

_____

_____

_____

Criminal Types

While there are countless types of criminals out there and varying degrees of crime, I am going to focus on the three most common types: rape, stalking, and murder. You will learn the different types of each of these attackers and become more familiar with behavioral patterns and actions you should be aware of.

She Asked for It

Rape. It is highly probable that you know someone who has been a victim of rape. It is the biggest criminal threat that women face, and it is the most personal. While most rape victims are female, males are not excluded from being a part of victim demographics. According to the *Findings from the National Violence Against Women Survey* published by the U.S. Department of Justice, about 3 percent of men have experienced attempted or completed rape.

Sadly, as far as we've come in supporting the women's movement and speaking out on behalf of violence against women, rape still carries lingering whispers of "Maybe she asked for it" or, especially in the case of acquaintance or date rape, "C'mon, she wanted it." This stigma creates a fear among raped women that hinders their need to personally address the situation, report the crime, and share their experience with those they love. It is nothing but unfortunate.

Perhaps the high incidence of rape somewhat diminishes the violent and serious nature of the crime, creating an attitude of apathy when another rape has been highlighted on the news. In order to recognize the serious impact rape has on its victims, the National Violence Against Women

---

FAST FACTS

- In 2002, there were 247,730 reported victims of rape, attempted rape, or sexual assault.
- One out of every six American women and one out of every thirty-three American men has been the victim of rape or attempted rape.
- Approximately 66 percent of rape victims know their assailant.
- Approximately 48 percent of victims are raped by a friend or acquaintance; 30 percent by a stranger; 16 percent by an intimate; and 2 percent by another relative. In 4 percent of cases, the relationship is unknown.

National Crime Victimization Survey, 2002,
and *National Violence Against Women Survey, 2000*

Prevention Research Center has published a study detailing the physical and emotional repercussions experienced by victims.

- Almost a third of rape victims develop post-traumatic stress disorder (PTSD), a debilitating mental disorder.
- Rape victims were five and a half times more likely to have current PTSD than those who had never been victims of crime (11 percent versus 2 percent).
- One-third of all rape victims seriously thought about committing suicide.
- Rape victims were thirteen times more likely than nonvictims to have attempted suicide.

FAST FACTS

- Almost two-thirds of rapes and sexual assaults occurred at night, between 6 PM and 6 AM.
- About seven in ten female rape or sexual assault victims stated that the offender was an intimate partner, spouse, other relative, friend, or acquaintance.

National Crime Victimization Survey
(Washington, DC: Bureau of Justice Statistics, 2003)

Incidences of rape occur frequently. The experience is traumatic, debilitating, and somewhat shameful. It is not to be taken lightly merely because it happens all the time.

As in general criminal profiling, it is impossible to point out a random person and say that he is or could become a rapist. However, there are some general qualities exhibited by rapists that seem to cross the board in profiling and can be seen in each of the four types of rapists I will discuss below. These include: sexualizing their relationships, low self-esteem, highly self-centered and insensitive attitudes regarding the feelings and thoughts of others, obsessive tendencies, substance abuse, excessive anger, and mood swings. Additionally, it is easier to distinguish sexually suspicious behavior in date or acquaintance rapists given the relational proximity. Because the woman is with a man in the acquaintance sense, she can pick up on strange vibes and signs. Most rapists who sexually assault people they know or are familiar with:

- Treat women with little to no respect.
- Drink heavily.
- Seem highly sexually active and physically and verbally aggressive.

- Don't understand that no means no.
- Display inappropriate fits of rage or jealousy.

The Four Types of Rapists

While sexual offenders vary in their personality traits, type of victim, motivations, and intent, the FBI has established four basic types of rapists, and has specified the motivations and behavior historically characteristic to each group. Not every offender will fall exclusively into one of the categories; he may display characteristics from more than one category.

• **The power reassurance rapist.** This is the most common type of rapist, representing approximately 40 percent of rape cases. Most acquaintance or date rapes fall into this category because the assailant is opportunistic and generally does not target his victim. He does not intend to kill or severely injure his victim, but tends to rape because of his need to compensate for sexual inadequacy and insecurity. Law enforcement authorities usually refer to him as the "gentleman rapist," though this is a clear example of an oxymoron. He tends to be delusional in thinking his victim has asked for and enjoyed the sexual attack. He usually operates within his geographic comfort zone to heighten his sense of security, so his victims either live or work in the same area as he does.

• **The power assertive (exploitative) rapist.** This type exhibits aggressive, dominating, and supermacho behavior. He has no insecurities about his masculine image and is extremely confident about his approach. He does not care about the victim at all and uses sexual abuse as a way to reinforce his masculinity. He selects women his own age and typically spends time targeting victims. He is physically violent and will tear clothing, enjoying the victim's physical and emotional humiliation.

• **The anger retaliator rapist.** This type is pretty self-explanatory. He has an overwhelming amount of pent-up negative emotion as a result of traumatic, humiliating, or abusive experiences with women in his past—his mother, an ex-girlfriend, and so on. He gets back at them by raping women. He rapes on an opportunistic basis, and his attacks are brutal. He will often beat his victims and humiliate them further with forced sodomy. His demeanor is explosive, his temper volatile, and he is very verbally abusive. It is not unusual for this person to be in a relationship with the woman he is abusing.

• **The anger excitation (sadistic) rapist.** This is the least common but most brutal rapist; his attacks are, in the majority of cases, fatal. His mission is to act out his sadistic fantasies on his prey. He can come across as seductive and charming, but derives his sexual stimulation and general excitement from watching his victims in pain. He will keep his victim from a few hours to a few days, thereby lengthening a victim's torture to his satisfaction.

The Stalker: Flattering, Annoying, or Dangerous?

Mention the word *stalking* and celebrities, political figures, and household names will probably come to mind. President Reagan, Brad Pitt, Madonna, and David Letterman are a handful of famous people you probably remember who have experienced stalking pests. Perhaps the most memorable celebrity stalking victim is Rebecca Schaeffer, the actress in the hit 1980s sitcom *My Sister Sam*. A fan obsessed with her beauty, talent, and rising-star quality took his fixation with Schaeffer too far when he shot and killed her in 1989. She was only twenty-two years old. This incident prompted the governor of California to pass the first antistalking legislation in the country, which later became the model for the rest of the country to follow.

But who would want to stalk a regular person? Where is the glamour in that? We're all too boring, right? Wrong. Stalking is a bigger problem for ordinary citizens than for movie stars. Most often, a stalker is known

---

FAST FACTS

- One out of every twelve women will be stalked during her lifetime.
- One out of every forty-five men will be stalked during his lifetime.
- Each year, 1,006,970 women are stalked.
- Each year, 370,990 men are stalked.
- The average duration of stalking behavior is 1.8 years. If a relationship between stalker and victim was or is present, this behavior lasts an average of 2.2 years.

National Institute of Justice,
*Stalking in America: Findings from
the National Violence Against Women Survey*
(Washington, DC: Department of Justice, 1998)

---

by the victim, whether an ex-husband, ex-boyfriend, or an acquaintance. The obsessive interest may seem innocent at first—perhaps an ex-boyfriend who wants his girlfriend back or someone at work who sends you flowers and chocolates — but can lead to physical violence, and even death.

There is no set module for characterizing the different types of stalkers, but there are three basic categories developed by Dr. Michael Zona from the University of Southern California School of Medicine.

• **Simple obsession.** This is the most prevalent form of stalking and usually stems from a prior relationship between the stalker and victim. The stalker experiences an overwhelming sense of rejection, which leads to anger, obsession, and a desire for retribution.

• **Love obsession.** This type of stalker usually has no relationship with a victim but has developed a fixation in his mind. The stalker believes he is truly in love with his victim.

IT'S PROBABLY SOMEONE YOU KNOW

- Eighty-one percent of women stalked by a current or former intimate partner are also physically assaulted by that partner.
- Thirty-one percent of women stalked by a current or former intimate partner are also sexually assaulted by that partner.
- Intimate partners who stalk are four times more likely than intimate partners in the general population to physically assault their victims and six times more likely to sexually assault their victims.
- Seventy-three percent of intimate partner stalkers verbally threaten the victims with physical violence, and almost 46 percent of victims experienced one or more violent incidents by the stalker.

National Institute of Justice,
*Stalking in America: Findings from
the National Violence Against Women Survey*
(Washington, DC: Department of Justice, 1998)

- **Erotomania.** This is similar to the love-obsessed stalker. The stalker believes that his victim is in love with him. The victim is usually a prominent figure in society, whether a well-known sports figure or a celebrity.

How do you know if you might be a victim of possible stalking? Here are some guidelines to help you recognize potential warning signs. If only one or two points relate to your situation, there is normally no need to worry. When almost all of the following conditions mirror what you are going through, you should start to seriously consider taking action, specifically alerting your local authorities.

- The person will not take no for answer. His mind is made up and there is nothing you can do or say to convince him otherwise.

- The person displays obsessive behavior. He is interested in what you do, when you do it, and how you do it.
- The person exhibits an excessive amount of the following emotions: jealousy, anger, guilt, frustration.
- The person has an obsessive personality.
- The person randomly shows up on a regular basis in places you frequent.
- You are receiving an unusually high number of prank or hang-up phone calls.
- You are receiving continuous and unwelcome gifts.
- The person is somewhat antisocial and has few or no personal relationships with friends and family.

MORE THAN INNOCENT OBSESSION

- Fifteen percent of the time, the stalker threatened or attempted to harm the victim, and 10 percent of the time, the stalker forced or attempted sexual contact.[1]
- The prevalence of anxiety, insomnia, social dysfunction, and severe depression is much higher among stalking victims than the general population, especially if the stalking involves being followed or having property destroyed.[2]
- Twenty-six percent of stalking victims lost time from work as a result of their victimization, and 7 percent never returned to work.
- Thirty percent of female victims and 20 percent of male victims sought psychological counseling.[3]

---

1. Bonnie S. Fisher, Francis T. Cullen, and Michael G. Turner, *The Sexual Victimization of College Women* (Washington, DC: National Institute of Justice, December 2000).

2. Blaaus, et al., "The Toll of Stalking," *Journal of Interpersonal Violence* 17, no. 1 (2002).

3. *Stalking in America: Findings from the National Violence Against Women Survey* (Washington, DC: Department of Justice, 1998).

Those Who Kill

Jack the Ripper. Son of Sam. Ted Bundy. Jeffrey Dahmer. Not only are they brutal, deranged, and perverse people, but they are household names as well. Most of us think of the word *murder* in a serial or mass sort of way, as multiple homicides that draw most of the media attention and create a state of frenzy and fear. Serial killings are scary to imagine, but the positive note is that they rarely occur.

The biggest fear that should arise from reading and studying homicide statistics is that in most cases the offender is an acquaintance. According to national statistics, the victim-offender relationship was revealed to investigative authorities in 55.5 percent of total murder cases. Within that percentage, 77.6 percent of the victims knew their assailant; only 22.4 percent of offenders were complete strangers. While you cannot absolutely eliminate yourself as a potential victim of random homicide, you can raise your awareness about potentially violent, volatile, or abusive relationships when it comes to people with whom you do associate.

FAST FACTS

- In 2003, the murder rate was estimated at 5.7 offenses per 100,000 U.S. inhabitants (a total of 16,503 homicides), an increase of 0.7 percent when compared with 2002 data.
- Ninety-one percent of murder victims were age eighteen or older.
- Seventy-eight percent of victims in 2003 were male; 22 percent were female.

2003 FBI Uniform Crime Report

Types of Murder

Single homicides occur for a variety of reasons. Some murderers are motivated by a reaction to something—a fight, an argument, basically any volatile situation where tempers flare and actions become uncontrollable. These can include domestic homicides and barroom brawls gone bad. Another major motivating factor is gain—the death of someone will result in the acquiring of money, power, fame, and so on. These can include assassinations of presidents and murders to collect insurance money.

Multiple murders fall into three basic categories and encompass many of the more famous homicides. They are the least likely to occur in your lifetime.

- **The serial killer.** A person who attacks and kills victims one by one in a series of incidents. These include Ted Bundy, Jeffrey Dahmer, and Edmund Kemper.
- **The spree killer.** A serial killer whose murders occur in a very short span of time, in two or more locations, and follow no discernible pattern. These include Bonnie and Clyde, and the Port Arthur Massacre.
- **The mass murderer.** A person, especially a political or military leader, who is responsible for the deaths of many individuals. These include the Heaven's Gate cult, the killings from the 9/11 tragedy, and the Jonesboro massacre.

What Makes a Killer

In Jonathan Pincus's book *Base Instincts: What Makes Killers Kill?*, he reflects on his research of studying the brains of murderers in trying to answer the question *Why do people kill?* He suggests that there are usually three underlying factors that converge to create the unstoppable urge to kill.

These factors are:

- Mental illness.
- Neurological damage.
- Child abuse.

Criminal profiling authority John Douglas notes two prevailing aspects of the personalities of countless numbers of violent offenders he has studied: superiority and inadequacy. Most felt they were smarter and more clever than anyone else. Their sheer existence put them above the law and societal norms, and they subsequently demanded their exceeding aptitude be recognized. In a similarly strong way, they felt extremely inadequate. Nothing they did was right. They couldn't please anyone; they couldn't get a job done.

Critical Points to Remember

First of all, the main mission in a criminal's life is to dominate, control, and manipulate. Criminals use helpless victims to carry out their goals by raping, assaulting, and murdering them. They don't care about your well-being. They don't care why you think you shouldn't be raped, attacked, or murdered. They have only one thing on their mind—you as their victim. They want to destroy, humiliate, and harm you. You should see this as an opportunity for permitting yourself to utilize self-defense if you find yourself in a physically compromising situation. It may be your only escape.

Second, note that victims are chosen three ways:

- **Randomly.** Who knows why? You have the least amount of control in this type of situation and have no viable offensive action to take. Your best bet is to use defensive action: physical self-defense.

• **Opportunely.** You are at the wrong place at the wrong time. A criminal has the uncontrollable urge to kill or rape and you happen to cross his path.

• **Selectively.** This is where a criminal stalks his victim. He watches what time she leaves her home in the morning and when she gets back. He determines where and when she shops, where and when she jogs, where and when she gets her morning coffee. He follows her routine and pattern and bases his opportunity to strike on what he knows about her schedule. The best way for you to gain offensive control is in changing habits. Switch the places you typically get your morning coffee. Change the route you use to get to work. Come home later or earlier; grocery shop at a different time or place. The less routine a criminal sees, the less likely he is to choose you as a victim.

Part II

Physical Self-Defense

6

When and How to Use Self-Defense

You read the statistics in the first part of this book, and you know that you are not impervious to crime. You've learned that self-defense is more mentally driven than physical. Hopefully, you are more aware of your surroundings, pay extra attention to your intuition, and know that you have the ability to execute effective self-defense.

Still, there are criminals out there walking our streets, prowling our communities, and attacking innocent victims without warning. It is my sincere hope that you will never be in a situation where self-defense is the only available exit strategy. It is my prayer that you never come face-to-face with a person who decides your fate rests in his hands because he has specifically chosen you or you happen to be at the wrong place at the wrong time. Furthermore, it is my responsibility to educate and equip you with simple physical techniques that can save your life should you ever encounter such an unfortunate situation.

Throughout my twenty-plus years of teaching self-defense, I have focused primarily on scenario-driven training. I have asked men and women all over the country what their worst fears are involving attacks. I role-play the criminal in each of those scenarios and show my students, step by step, what they need to be aware of during an attack and how they can defend themselves.

Obviously, you could find yourself in any of countless threatening situations; no two attacks are identical. For simplicity's sake and to ensure you receive a solid understanding of these techniques, I have used scenarios that people typically fear and that do occur in this day and age. A lot of the same moves are used in the different situations because these defenses are equally uncomplicated, versatile, and effective. You'll find no mention of fancy kicks, techniques, gimmicks, or difficult moves requiring an extensive amount of coordination. Remember, self-defense is *not* used to fight; it's used to defend. An attack is not a wrestling or sparring match, so these methods have been created for the sole purpose of incapacitating your attacker long enough for you to escape.

Below are some key points to think about before you read on and learn the moves. Let this information sink in as much as possible. You will gain a better understanding of its importance as you read the subsequent self-defense scenarios, which incorporate these concepts in greater detail.

Surprise! What Makes This Work

Remember, there are no guarantees. No one can promise you that learning any form of self-defense will let you escape any and every dangerous situation. What I can guarantee is that the techniques do work. It is possible to take down a man twice your size by strategically maneuvering his wrist a certain way. You can undermine an attacker's intimidating use of a weapon by controlling the weapon away from where it is being pointed at your body. The secret is in surprise.

Think about it.

A criminal attack usually happens without warning. You have zero seconds to prepare. There is nothing leading up to the attack. This is why most people are easy prey. The surprise element usually makes a victim panic, feel fearful, and ultimately freeze or become hysterical. A criminal expects his victim to respond by screaming or flailing about. While screaming works in drawing attention, it won't help if there is no one around to listen. Kicking, punching, or scratching without having a target in mind only wastes energy. These two things are what a criminal is waiting for and will make his attempts at attacking you successful.

You need to turn the tables on an attacker. The best thing to do if you are attacked is to remain calm by controlling your fear. Instead of letting the panic overwhelm you to the point of paralysis, understand that what is happening is real and that you have no choice but to defend yourself. You can fight back or become another victim of crime. By striking back opportunely, you will throw an attacker off-guard because he does not expect you to know how to defend yourself. What he expects is screaming, crying, and aimless punches. When you do strike in self-defense, *his* reaction time immediately slows down significantly. You make him vulnerable and buy yourself time to get away.

Nonphysical Self-Defense

Self-defense does not solely comprise physical defensive techniques. Before situations escalate to the physical level, there are usually numerous things that happen to warn you of such danger. It is during this period that you are indirectly given some choices on how to approach the situation, whether you realize it or not. Not all potentially threatening situations need to move past verbal altercations or even walking away to avoid them entirely. Below are some things you need to be aware of on your continued journey in learning self-defense. When is simple confrontation enough? When is compliance appropriate? When should you just walk away?

Let's find out.

Confront the Situation

If you are in a possibly threatening situation with another person or are in an environment where you suddenly become uncomfortable, you can do something about it—and you should. Red flags that start going off in your head are indicators of some type of alarm, whether it's something mildly wrong or potentially life threatening. Let's say you are car shopping, browsing through the plethora of vehicles in an outdoor auto mall. You feel as if someone is watching and following you. You feel as though holes are being bored into your head from a stare. Out of the corner of your eye, you can see a person standing a couple of feet away from you looking at you in a peculiar fashion. No matter how far or where you move, he is on your trail, though in a subtle manner.

What do you do? Do you just ignore your discomfort and continue car shopping as if nothing is happening? Do you pretend nothing is wrong? No. If you don't feel right, something isn't right and you have the responsibility to yourself to make the situation comfortable. You should turn right around, walk up to him, and say, "Hey, can I help you with something? I noticed you've been following me around. Do I know you?" Don't be afraid or too timid to address your concerns. If the person *has* been following you around, chances are, he'll leave you alone. Why? Because you have made yourself aware of his presence and let him know that you know he's there. Awareness and confrontation, when necessary, are a great formula for staying safe.

Draw Attention

Like confrontation, drawing attention is another great way to ward off possibly dangerous people. When you are in a location where there are other people present, you have been given an ideal environment for creating drama. Let's say you are on vacation and touring the attractions with a group of girlfriends. You are walking down a populated street admiring the jewelry, clothing, and trinkets decorating stores' window displays when a group of guys start moving toward you, harassing you with verbal and physical threats. What do you do? You need to draw attention to the commotion, and you can do this in a couple of different ways. Since you're in a crowded street, you can confront the group of men and ask them what their problem is. You do this in a loud voice so everyone will hear. This will draw attention to this situation; people will stare and, even more likely, people will come to your aid and find out what is wrong. You can also go into one of the stores and tell a manager, customer, or worker that the guys are bothering you.

Other people will be made aware of their behavior, and it will probably be stopped immediately. Nobody wants to look like a fool or a bad guy in front of people. It's embarrassing to them, and that type of attention is negative and definitely not in their favor.

Walk the Other Way

There are times when we unconsciously walk right into a dangerous situation . . . whether we are distracted by something or because we think we can handle it. This is a big no-no. Why put yourself in danger when you don't have to?

I've been trained in martial arts ever since I was a teenager. I have worked with law enforcement officials and members of the FBI and SWAT teams for more than twenty years. I stay in shape by working out almost every day. I am saying all of this not to brag, but to make a point— when it comes to defending myself, I feel pretty confident I can take care of myself. However, if I were walking in a park and saw a group of guys a couple of yards away who just looked like they were up to no good, what do you think I would do? Would I walk past them with a cocky attitude as if to say *Bring it on*? Would I provoke their attention by calling them out? No. I would walk the other way and avoid the situation entirely. Why? Do I think I'm a wimp or afraid? Of course not. But I do understand that the best way to avoid possible trouble is by not walking into a situation simply because I can. There are times when walking away will leave you in a better place because you made the right choice.

Play the Actor

I worked in several big cities as a bouncer for many years and have dealt with one too many belligerent and drunk individuals. My strategy in getting them to remain calm worked every time. No, I didn't throw them out of the clubs with my bare hands. Nor did I punch their lights out to teach them a lesson. I'm sure you've heard the expression "Kill them with kindness"; well, that is exactly what I did. I've had guys who were intoxicated beyond belief and consequently acting out in a rude, hot-tempered, and aggressive manner. Instead of playing tough guy, I simply walked over to them and began to talk to them in a calm and kind fashion. I'd reassure them that they were okay and that everyone has gotten that drunk at some point in their lives . . . no problem! I'd bribe them—I'd ask them to drink some coffee and then say I'd buy them a beer later. What happened? They calmed down. They responded to kindness better than if I'd started yelling and manhandling them in an effort to control them.

The same strategy can work with people who are exhibiting erratic and crazy behavior. If you're not a medical expert or police officer, it may be difficult to tell if folks are on drugs, are drunk, or are mentally ill. The bottom line, however, is that they are acting out of control and you cannot predict their future actions. If you are approached by people who appear to be maniacal, don't set them off by showing them you have immediately powered on your defense mode. Talk to them in a calm manner, ask them what is wrong, and see if you can help. The only time you need to employ physical self-defense is if they take that route first.

Only When Necessary

Self-defense is not something any individual should take lightly. There are repercussions that result from severely striking an attacker. You use self-defense when you have no choice. If you are mugged, your purse is stolen, and the guy is running off with it leaving you empty-handed, what do you do? Should you run after him to reclaim your goods? Do you chase and catch the bad guy to teach him a lesson or two? No. You should do nothing except report the criminal activity to the police. Any form of physical defense should be used only when your life is in danger and you have no way of escaping. You fight back to gain the time you need to escape. That's it.

You need to use intuition, common sense, and diligence in assessing a threat level.

- Do you feel your life is in danger? Is the guy strangling you, trying to rape you, or brandishing a lethal weapon before your eyes?
- Does he seem reasonable to verbally negotiate with? Can you escape by any other means than using force?
- Do you have any other means of escape than physically weakening his advances? Can you run toward the company of other people? Can you move toward an open place of business and get immediate help?

If you are in a situation where violent behavior is being instigated by someone you are familiar with, you need to use extreme caution in assessing the level of threat. If your date is trying to grope you, or your boss is putting his hand where it doesn't belong, forceful verbiage and body language need to be incorporated first and foremost. Saying no and backing away is generally enough defensive action for these types of scenarios. These are not life-threatening situations.

However, threats are automatically heightened if someone is trying to tear your shirt off, is placing a knife on your throat, or is manhandling you. Use your intuition, common sense, and diligence in assessing what might be dangerous behavior.

Compliance or Physical Self-Defense?

One of the most frequently asked questions in my workshops is what to do when you are threatened and forced to give up something . . . whether it be your wallet, purse, or other valuable belonging. If you have a gun pointed to your head and a criminal asks for your wallet, do you give up your wallet or fight back? Where is that line drawn?

Because none of us is God, or a psychic, or blessed with ESP, we absolutely do not know how far a criminal will go after the initial threat. Maybe we won't get raped if we give him our watch. Maybe we won't be killed if we hand a criminal the keys to our car. On the other hand, maybe we will. There are no guarantees.

In my experience, however, I have created some general rules to live by. There are times when it is better to give up something in return for possibly preserving your life, and there are other times when you have no alternative but to fight for your life.

Give It Up

If you are with someone else—your child, your spouse, your friend, your mother—and someone tries to threaten you, give him what he wants. Not only do you have to defend yourself, but now there is another variable in the equation—another human being. Being concerned about yourself is one thing, but when there is someone else to think about, the risk is just too great. If you are by yourself, you can defend yourself faster and easier, but it's much more complicated when someone else is with you. It's a chance I wouldn't suggest taking.

If you are being threatened and there is no weapon in sight, your best option is to give the attacker what he wants. Normally threats are initiated by weapons or physical moves, and in that case, you have no choice but to defend yourself. But if a young man comes up to you, his hands—which are without any weapons—are in plain sight, he is not touching you, and he asks for your wallet "or else," give him your wallet.

Fight Back

The most obvious call for self-defense is if someone grabs you, touches you, or makes any physical moves that are harmful. If you fear for your life, you need to protect it.

If you are approached by a person carrying a weapon, you must fight back if the weapon is on you. If you can feel a gun or knife on your back, head, or any part of your body, don't give in. Giving him what he wants only puts the ball in his court, and now he has the opportunity to do whatever he wants with you . . . he can shoot you, rape you, or injure you in some way.

If there is a distance between you and the weapon, you need to wait for the right moment to strike (closing the gap will be discussed in greater detail in chapter 8). You should let your attacker figure out what the next step is going to be. You can fight back most effectively when he is close and when you can see and feel the weapon.

When You Have No Choice

Finally, before you continue reading how to perform physical self-defense, you need to understand the most important item. Only use self-defense if you feel your life is in imminent danger and you have no other option of escape.

The moves you will learn in this part of the book are not for the faint of heart and can be deadly. This is to emphasize the true meaning and appropriate use of self-defense. The scenarios used depict self-defense techniques that are executed in life-threatening situations *only*. If some drunken guy in a bar won't stop talking to you and is putting his hands all over you, get a bouncer to take control of him. Do not gouge his eye out. If you are at an office holiday function and your boss starts to make sexually inappropriate comments and tries to put his hand on your thigh, don't strike his throat, walk away.

- Self-defense *is not* a physical way to show how cool, strong, or tough you are.
- Self-defense *is not* to be used when you can walk or run away or verbally defend yourself.
- Self-defense is to be used *only* if your life is threatened and you have no other option to get away.

7

Know Your Target

Knowing the particulars of self-defense includes not only setting a positive mind-set for yourself, but additionally becoming acquainted with the human body. Specifically, I am referring to general target areas on a human body that have the greatest amount of exposure and vulnerability.

When you find yourself in a situation where self-defense is necessary, you need to strike the areas that will weaken an attacker to the greatest degree. By focusing your defensive actions on the most vulnerable areas rather than throwing blind punches, you gain the time you need to escape and get help. Your survival is dependent not on the amount of strength you have, but on your knowledge and understanding of where and how to debilitate your attacker. Remember, you are fighting his weaknesses, not his strengths.

Which action, propelled by an average person, do you think would result in the most physical injury to another—striking someone with full force on his arm or striking a person's throat from a few inches away? The answer is the latter. This is another clear example of the strong not always having domination over the weak. It's not in how big or physically powerful you are, but in what you know and how you use that knowledge. If you learn where to strike an attacker's body so his strength is physically crippled, you can defend yourself against someone who may look like a WWE wrestler. Size and strength are little to no advantage to him when you can see where his weakness is and use it against him.

The Groin—Overexposed and Highly Overrated

The most basic form of defensive action that the majority of women seem to propose is to "Kick him where it hurts." Hmmm . . . getting kicked in that highly sensitive area for a man is definitely no picnic, and it definitely does hurt. But is it effective enough to debilitate an attacker's advances so you are afforded the time you need to escape? Not necessarily.

You have to remember that most guys already know this is the number one area their victims will look to defensively attack. Men are instinctively protective of their groin. And technically, in order to debilitate a man by striking this area, you have to penetrate it with more force than you can imagine. Think about it. The attacker is already on somewhat of a euphoric high from trying to attack you, so a strike to that area will not be as powerful as striking a specific target point. A man can easily recover from getting kicked in the groin, but less so when he is struck on a weaker point on the body. The key to remember in executing self-defense is to use physical techniques that don't allow for an easy recovery. You need to weaken the attacker so severely, he physically cannot retaliate.

Additionally, the majority of attacks occur after you are initially grabbed. In that physical position, you generally have defensive access to the upper half of your and his bodies, rather than the lower half. That being said, strikes to the upper area will be physically easier to execute. I'm not suggesting that strikes in the groin region will not work in defending yourself. (If you are steadfast in using this approach, here's a little word to the wise: When you target this area, drive your strike upward.)

The bottom line is that anything you can do to escape works for me and, more important, for you. However, there are alternative spots that are easier to access and strike, and are more likely to be effective in disabling your attacker. What I'm going to show you are the three main target areas you can approach that generally work best in self-defense.

The Big Three

The top three parts of a body that are usually most exposed and vulnerable during an attack are the eyes, the throat, and the pelvis. These are the areas that are most likely to be accessible to a victim. Strikes executed to these areas at a close range will cause significant and severe injury—what you need to be able to get away and get help. The next chapter will discuss effective strikes to these and other target areas in greater detail.

The Eyes

Striking an eye or two may not be a pretty picture to paint, but when you are in a vulnerable situation, you don't have many options in your favor. The eyes are one of the best targets for self-defense tactics because (1) they are easy to find; (2) they are almost always exposed; and (3) striking them causes a great deal of pain and injury. Strikes to this area can cause blindness, the eye bulb to rupture, or an eyelid to tear.

There are several different ways to strike the eye to debilitate a person. Use both of your thumbs (your thumbprint area) to wipe your attacker straight across the eye area. This will make his eyes significantly water. You can also strike your fingers straight into the eye area or rake your fingernails straight across the eyes. Additionally, you can drive your thumbs straight into the inner corner of the attacker's eyes. If you have keys or another sharp object in your hands, you can use that item to execute the same action (see Figure 7.1).

Striking the Eye
Figure 7.1

The Throat

The throat is one of the most sensitive areas on the body. Any form of physical assault to the side or front areas of the throat area will be powerful. A strike to the front of the throat could crush the larynx or esophagus, leaving someone unable to breathe. A strike to the side of the throat, slightly above the collarbone, can cause severe damage to both the jugular vein and carotid artery. Other injuries can result from blows, including contusions of major veins, fractures, and suffocation due to damage of breathing passageways. The three main anatomical parts of the throat that can be severely damaged during this process are:

• **The larynx.** Commonly known as the voice box, it contains the vocal chords and is the air passageway between the pharynx and the trachea. The larynx is located right above the trachea. It is two inches long and shaped like a tube. If you place your finger right under your Adam's apple and hum, you should be able to feel your vocal chords vibrating; voilà, you have found your larynx!

• **The trachea.** This is commonly referred to as the windpipe and is located right below the larynx. It is the long tube going down your throat right underneath the layers of skin and the main airway to the lungs. If you apply pressure to your throat anywhere on the trachea, you will experience tremendous difficulty in breathing and a lot of pain. Now just imagine how badly you can weaken an attacker if you strike this area at full force!

• **The esophagus.** It is located right behind the trachea and is the passageway for swallowing your food and drinks. You will not be able to feel it on the outside of your neck.

The Pelvis

It is important to understand that the pelvic area and the groin are not the same thing; most people get the two confused. Your pelvis is a basin-shaped structure of bones that supports the weight of your upper body (see Figure 7.2). Commonly referred to as your hip bones, the two major bones in your pelvis are your coccyx bones. The pelvis begins right underneath the top formation of your pubic hair, below the belly button. If you press your fingers into that area, you should be able to feel the bony region.

Pelvic Area
Figure 7.2

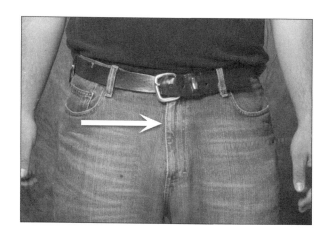

It takes about eighteen pounds of pressure to break a bone. The pelvis is one of the most vulnerable areas because of the major bones that it comprises. If an average 150-pound woman strikes the pelvic bone with full force, it will break.

Other Targets

The human body is full of vulnerable areas vital for use as targets in self-defense in addition to the eyes, throat, and pelvic region. Some are obvious; others are not. As these target areas are defined and depicted, take a few moments to feel where they are located on your own body. Apply light pressure to these points—please don't hurt yourself—and you will directly experience how sensitive they really are. Any form of striking may cause significant and traumatic injuries. Use this knowledge as another reminder that self-defense should only be used when necessary—when your life is in danger and you have no other way to escape.

The Head and Neck Region

• **Temples.** If you put your hands to the sides of your forehead (see Figure 7.3) and clench your teeth a few times, you'll feel a movement in your head each time you clench. This is the exact spot of your temples. Any blows to that area of the head will hurt tremendously and might even render an attacker unconscious. Try pressing your fingers in your temple area and you'll experience the pain brought on by even the lightest pressure.

• **Ears.** Cupping both of your attacker's ears with your hands and clapping them with your palms is extremely powerful (see Figure 7.4). His eardrums may burst, and he may sustain a concussion.

Temples
Figure 7.3

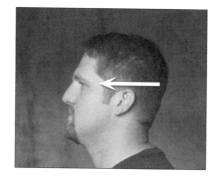

Cupping the Ears
Figure 7.4

- **Nose.** The bridge of the nose is the most vulnerable area of that body part. Striking it will likely cause your attacker to be unable to breathe and break bones in that area.
- **Philtrum.** This is the midline groove running from the bottom of your nose to the indentation in your upper lip (see Figure 7.5). You can strike this area or use your finger to push this area and ultimately push back an attacker's head in an attempt to get him out of your space. Try placing your finger on this area and pushing hard; you'll see how sensitive it is. Damage to this area may result in a split lip, chipped or cracked teeth, or unconsciousness.
- **Maxillary sinuses.** These are located right under your eye, at the top of your cheeks (see Figure 7.6). A blow to this area may shatter them.

Philtrum
Figure 7.5

Maxillary Sinuses
Figure 7.6

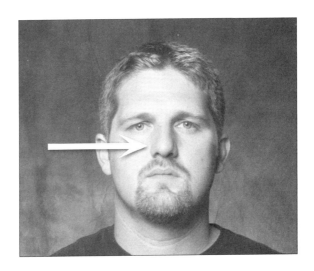

• **Frontal sinus.** A large cavity located above the eyebrows (see Figure 7.7). A lot of headaches erupt from this sensitive area.

• **Jaw.** The most vulnerable area is the back of the jaw, just below the ear where the bone begins (see Figure 7.8). If you gently slap the edge of your palm against it, you'll notice the pain. Additionally, if you strike the jaw right in the center or underneath, you may be able to fracture bones in that area.

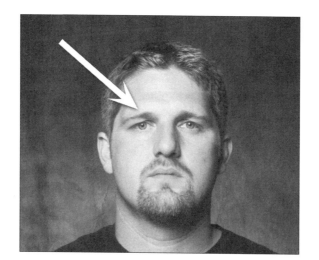

Frontal Sinus
Figure 7.7

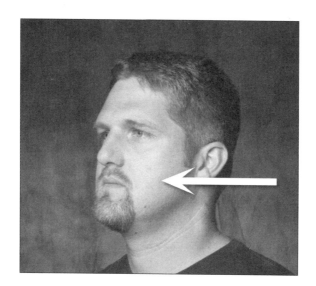

Vulnerable
Jaw Area
Figure 7.8

• **Carotid artery and jugular veins.** Both of these lie in the right side of the neck (see Figure 7.9) and are extremely susceptible to injury. If struck, swelling of the brain or a hematoma may occur, and possibly result in brain damage or even death. A good way to get the exact position of your carotid artery is to take your pulse, especially after performing some type of physical activity that gets your heart rate up. Using the second and third fingers of your hand, place them on either side of your neck where you feel a beating pulse. That is your carotid artery. The jugular veins run down the sides of the neck. They are located well within the neck area, so you can't feel them by simply touching your neck.

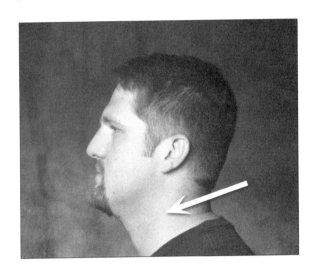

Carotid Artery
and Jugular Veins
Figure 7.9

• **Back of the neck.** If a blow is suffered at the point where the spine meets the skull (see Figure 7.10), it can knock out an attacker. It may also sever the spinal cord, which may result in paralysis or even death.

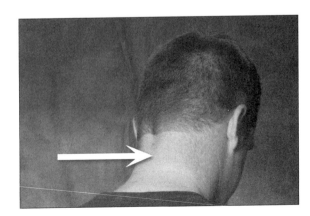

Vulnerable
Neck Point
Figure 7.10

The Upper Body

• **Sternum.** This is the breastbone, the center of the chest, which covers the heart (see Figure 7.11). A really heavy blow can break many ribs and cause someone to be unable to breathe.

Sternum
Figure 7.11

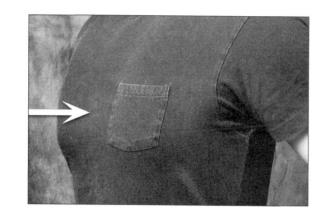

• **Solar plexus.** This is located in the upper middle of the abdomen just below the sternum (see Figure 7.12). Substantive force to this area can shock the nervous system and, consequently, limit or destroy an attacker's ability to breathe. People who have been struck in this area usually report "having the wind knocked out" of them.

Solar Plexus
Figure 7.12

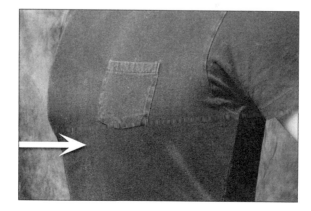

• **Floating ribs.** These are the shortest and lowest ribs at the side of the body (see Figure 7.13). They are very sensitive to finger or knuckle pressure. Striking this area is a great way to force an attacker to release you from a bear hug. A hard blow can break them, and there's a slight risk of puncturing a lung.

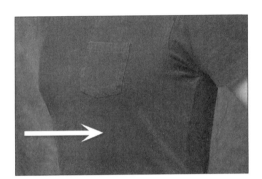

Floating Ribs
Figure 7.13

• **Side of the rib cage.** You can feel exactly where this is if you press your fingers about an inch down from your armpit on the side of your torso. It is a highly sensitive area, and blows to this area will hurt to a debilitating degree.

• **Biceps and triceps.** Striking the inside area between the bicep (see Figure 7.14) and tricep (see Figure 7.15) muscles causes debilitating pain.

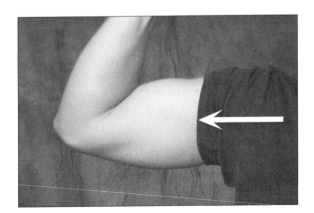

Biceps
Figure 7.14

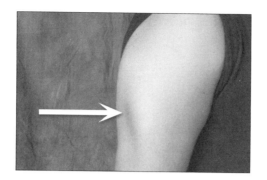

Triceps
Figure 7.15

• **Upper back.** Located on the spinal column halfway between the shoulder blades is a raised ridge area (see Figure 7.16). Striking this area can result in a loss of balance, pain, shock, and even spinal cord damage.

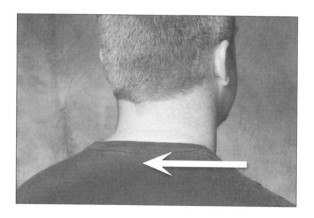

Upper Back
Figure 7.16

The Lower Body

• **Back of the knee.** Striking this area will immediately throw an attacker off-balance and possibly dislocate bones.
• **Side of the knee.** (see Figure 7.17) This area is most vulnerable, and provides access to the anterior cruciate ligament (ACL) located in the center of your knee.
• **Knee.** Striking either below or above the kneecap (see Figure 7.18) hits another vulnerable target area.

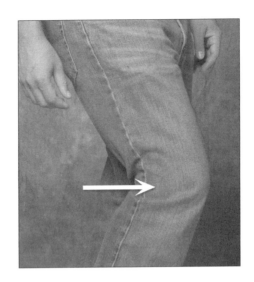

Side of
the Knee
Figure 7.17

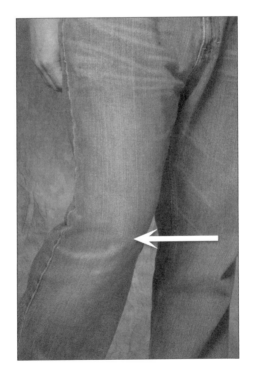

Kneecap
Figure 7.18

• **Groin.** (see Figure 7.19) Though I'd prefer striking an attacker in
the pelvic region rather than the groin any day, you can strike it in a cer-

Groin
Figure 7.19

tain way to weaken your attacker. Driving your strike straight up instead of hitting the groin head-on is more forceful.

Assessing Your Target

Forget About His Size

Clearly, there are many target areas on an attacker's body that you can strike in order to cause significant injury. His size is not the issue; your knowledge of his vital points is what is important. If you can understand where you are striking, how painful it can be, and the type of injury that can result from that blow, you can begin to appreciate self-defense as a practical and necessary means for survival. This is the crux of how you fight an attacker's weakness, not his strengths.

Take What You See

In the subsequent chapters, you'll hear this phrase again. What I mean by *Take what you see* is to strike a target area that you immediately see when your attacker is closing in on you. This target area has to be easily accessible and within your vision to ensure the accuracy of your strike. While I recommend that my students strike one or more, if necessary, of the big three target areas—the eyes, the throat, or the pelvis—sometimes they are not what you see first and, therefore, not readily available to strike. You may be lying on the ground and see his knees, in which case you would strike the sides of them to cause injury to his ACL, or strike the top of the knee, which would cause tendon damage and extreme pain.

Go Low

As you already know, one reason self-defense is so effective is that you turn the tables on the attacker just by using your self-protective techniques. You are surprising him with your ability to fight back. A criminal can't quite imagine that a victim will have any knowledge of the vital areas on his body vulnerable to extreme pressure. So when you strike any one of them, that jolt will throw him physically and mentally off-balance.

Another surprise tactic I like to use is striking the attacker in a low region; as I've mentioned, the pelvic area is one of my favorites. When you are attacked, and if it's physically possible, drop down immediately to the ground. To comprehend this visually, one of your knees will be directly on the ground and the other leg out to the side. In this position, your head will be parallel with the lower half of his body. Dropping low and striking an available target area will double the element of surprise. I will expand on some of these low techniques in the following chapter.

Understand the Severity of Injuring Target Areas

This cannot be emphasized enough. Self-defense is not to be used to show off, as a practical joke, to intimidate innocent people (specifically unassuming family members or annoying siblings), or to prove great physical strength and mental knowledge. The target areas mentioned above are described to you because they are the areas that will debilitate someone who is attacking you. You need to use your intuition and gauge your threat level before you consider striking these areas. Obviously, if you are being pushed, shoved, roughly manhandled, threatened with a weapon, or facing another serious threat, self-defense will be the option you need to use. Use self-defense techniques as a way to get out of a situation where your life is threatened.

Now that we've learned where to strike, let's move on and become educated in the correct methods of striking target areas.

8

Your Body,
Your Mind, Your Weapon

You don't own a gun, a knife, a rottweiler, or weapons of mass destruction. You don't have a superman boyfriend or a twenty-four-hour police escort. You may work out regularly—not enough to match the strength, speed, and agility of a triathlete, but enough to maintain your strong heart, high energy level, and relatively good shape. You consider yourself to be somewhat strong, confident, and, most important, aware. If you close your eyes for a moment and think about a situation where you're being attacked and your assailant is bigger, taller, and stronger than you, how do you think you would fare?

Would it be your strength training at the gym that would guide your self-defensive movements and enforce the strength and effectiveness of your actions? Would it be aimless flailing about of your extremities that would get you out of the situation—the hope that one of your arms might hit something vulnerable on the attacker's body? Would it be some fancy karate moves you saw on a martial arts movie that you try to replicate in an effort to save your life?

No. Thankfully, self-defense comprises simpler elements. You already know that understanding and believing the following statements is critical in learning, and ultimately performing, self-defense:

- Self-confidence is the first step in learning self-defense.
- Only you can give yourself the permission to fight back.
- Strength and power are developed from what you know, not how big or tough you are.
- You need to do whatever it takes to get out of a threatening situation alive.

In the last chapter, you were made aware of the most vulnerable areas to strike when using self-defense. You know the eyes, throat, and pelvic area should be the most sought-after targets. These target areas are not hard to find and will, most of the time, be visible and exposed for you to strike. But how do you use your body as a weapon? How do you strike these areas? What moves work the best? How hard should you strike?

As I've mentioned before, while there are a plethora of different striking, punching, and kicking techniques, learning all of them would be time consuming and require a tremendous amount of commitment and expertise. Not to mention, your brain would probably go into overload and, as a result, it would be difficult to remember even a few of them. In keeping self-defense both easy to learn and effective, I focus mainly on using specific target areas that are vulnerable as well as correlating striking moves that are easy to execute. These moves can be used in many different scenarios and situations.

Basic Types of Strikes

In martial arts, five basic strikes involve the use of your hand. Any of these five can be used in many different ways and many different scenarios. Different forms of martial arts and self-defense courses have other names for these techniques, but the techniques, in and of themselves, are the same. The next chapters will include scenarios using these techniques in self-defense, so it is best to really understand how each of them works and how to perform them all.

- Front punch
- Back fist
- Hammer blow
- Shuto strike
- Palm strike

Before we look at how to execute each of these strikes, here are some key points to remember to make a punch as powerful as possible:

- Make a fist with your hand. Your fingers should be curled in as tightly as possible so your fingernails dig into the meaty area of your palm. The thumb should be wrapped over and around your fingers. It should *not* be placed inside the fist or on the outside sticking straight up.
- The knuckles on your pointer and middle fingers should be sticking out farther than the others. These knuckles are the first point of impact your assailant should feel when you strike. They are used to penetrate the assailant.
- Punches should be thrown from the hips, using your lower body as your power source.
- Draw back a punch as fast as possible. You don't want your body to absorb the punch—that will lessen the power of the action. When you strike your target, do not let your fist linger in that area, pull it back immediately after striking.

Front Punch

This is the most common type of punch, and is used to strike head-on with the fist (specifically using the two major knuckles) (see Figure 8.1). Pull your arm back at your side, elbow bent. Then drive it straight forward toward your target. Right before impact, twist the wrist slightly to release the most amount of power. (More on this twisting power, known as torque, later.)

Front Punch
Figure 8.1

Back Fist

This punch uses the back of your fist and first two knuckles to strike (see Figure 8.2). Bend your elbow so your fingers are curled toward you and your fist is level with your nose. The power is drawn from flipping the wrist, which reinforces the hand.

Back Fist
Figure 8.2

Hammer Blow

This strike is similar to a punch in using a closed fist as described above, but the method of execution is different. Instead of using the front or back of your closed hand to deliver the hammer blow, you will be using the bottom of your fist, where your pinkie lies, to strike a target area (see Figure 8.3). The power to deliver this strike comes from the movement of the area between your elbow and your wrist. Think *sledgehammer.*

Shuto Strike

This is probably one of the most effective hand techniques, and you will notice a majority of my self-defense scenarios use this strike. Executed correctly, this strike is extremely powerful and debilitating against your attacker. The key element in this strike is its rigidity. Open your hand with your fingers extended and as close together as possible (see Figure 8.4). Bend and tuck your thumb into the palm of your hand (see Figure 8.5);

this is what will make the strike rigid and powerful. Strike your target with the edge of your hand where your pinkie is.

Hammer Blow
Figure 8.3

Shuto Strike:
Fingers
Extended
Figure 8.4

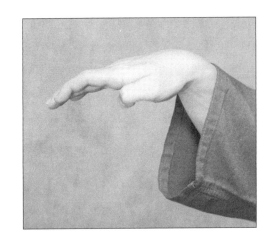

Shuto Strike:
Thumb Tuck
Figure 8.5

Palm Strike

Open your hand and put your fingers close together. Place your thumb next to your fingers, not folded into the palm. Curve the tips of your fingers in slightly while keeping the hand arched backward perpendicular to your wrist (see Figure 8.6). The heel of your palm should be pulled

Palm Strike
Figure 8.6

slightly more forward than your fingers to ensure that this area will strike first. Strike forward, twisting your wrist slightly prior to contact. It is important to use the heel of the hand to strike, rather than the entire palm.

Later in this chapter you will learn ways to practice these basic strikes in general as well as with specific target areas.

Other Simple Moves

Vertical Strikes

This move is similar to the shuto strike described above. Once again, your hand is flat, fingers tightly together, thumb tucked under your palm (see Figure 8.7). However, this time instead of striking your attacker's target

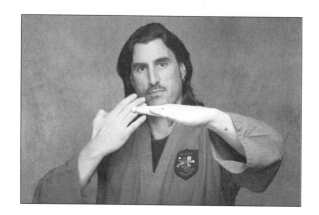

Vertical Strike:
Flat Hand
Figure 8.7

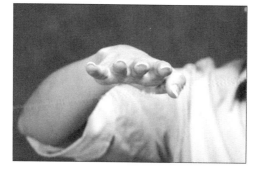

Vertical Strike:
Finger Use
Figure 8.8

area with the side edge of your hand, you will be striking using the ends of your second, third, and fourth fingers (see Figure 8.8). This is a great technique for striking any part of the throat.

Controlling Moves Using the Knee

If you have an attacker down, you can control him and keep him on the ground using your knee. This technique is useful if assistance, whether in the form of a police officer or a bystander, is running to your rescue. Prior to executing this move, you want to first weaken the attacker. Remember, you want to use the most debilitating defensive action that you can so the

Controlling
with Knee
Figure 8.9

Controlling
with Knee
Figure 8.10

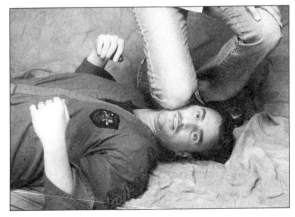

attacker is rendered physically useless. Strike his pelvis to break the bone, or strike the throat so he is unable to breathe—do something that will leave him physically unable to fight back. Once he is weakened and on the ground, drive your knee into his forehead (see Figure 8.9) or jaw (see Figure 8.10) and let it remain there using your full body weight. It will be almost impossible for him to get up.

Ear Cupping

As mentioned in the previous chapter, the ears are extremely vulnerable to being hit. Cup your hands, fingers curled slightly inward, and thumbs tightly pressed against your hand. Place your hands over each ear and quickly clap them against your attacker's ears using the same cupped position (see Figure 8.11). The most important aspect of this method is to cup the hands—it is the cupping technique, not your strength, that causes injuries.

Ear Cupping
Figure 8.11

Thumb Drive

The thumbs are powerful weapons. They are small, but strong. Use them mainly for striking the eye area. Wipe the entire eye area from side to side using your thumbs (see Figure 8.12), or drive your thumb into the inner corner of the attacker's eye. You can also rake the eye with your fingernails.

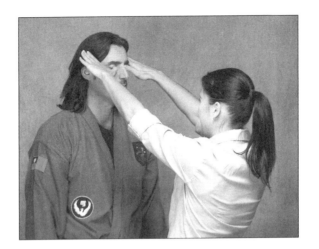

Thumb Drive
Figure 8.12

Going Low

In the last chapter, I discussed dropping down to the floor and striking your attacker from this position. One of my favorite moves in going low is to sweep an attacker off his feet. Drop down to the ground so your head is facing the lower half of his body. Then place both of your palms on the inside area of each of his ankles (see Figures 8.13 and 8.14). With force, pull his ankles forward, toward you, so that you literally pull his feet out

Going Low
Figure 8.13

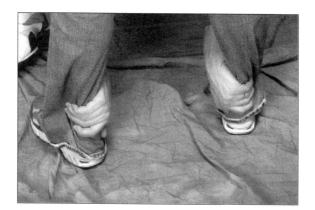

Going Low
Figure 8.14

from under him. He will be knocked off-balance and will fall back. This is a great move to use after you have weakened him by performing another debilitating self-defense technique. You weaken him first by striking any one of his target areas and then finish the move by taking away his balance.

Natural Weapons

Your body is a natural weapon. The basic techniques of striking mentioned above utilize mainly the hands. But what about the elbow or forearm? What are the parts of our bodies that can be manipulated and used when defending against an attacker?

Elbows

The beauty of your elbows is that they almost entirely consist of bones. What you want to remember is to use primarily the tip of the elbow (see Figure 8.15), which is the sharpest point. Strike your target area with the tip of your elbow hard and fast.

Elbow Use
Figure 8.15

Forearm

A forearm can be used to horizontally strike an attacker's neck. You can use this move with your arm either fully extended or bent at the elbow. If your back is facing the front of his body and you are moving into him that way, use the back of your forearm to deliver this strike. Step slightly to one side and use the back of your forearm—where the outside of your elbow is located—and strike under his chin. If you are facing him and moving toward him, strike him with the inside part of your forearm (see Figure 8.16)—where the inside of the elbow is.

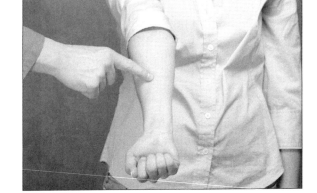

Inside Forearm
Figure 8.16

Knees

If your attacker's target areas are in close proximity, you may be very effective in striking one with your raised, bent knee (see Figure 8.17). You
can use a knee, depending on the situation and your physical position, to
strike the pelvis, throat, or other area on the body. It is particularly useful
if you have already weakened him somehow, and he is bent over. Kneeing
him in the face will further weaken him.

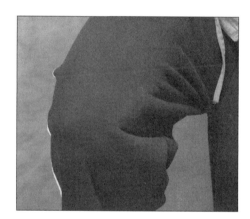

Knee Use
Figure 8.17

The Web of Your Hand

This is the area of your hand between the base of your thumb and your
pointer finger. Using this part of your hand is primarily effective in deliv-

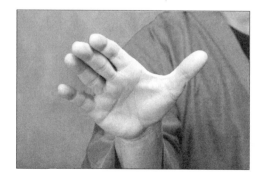

Hand Use
Figure 8.18

ering strikes to the throat. Make a V using your outstretched thumb as one edge and the rest of your fingers, drawn close together, as the other (see Figure 8.18). Strike the throat in that V shape, keeping both sides extremely rigid.

Fingers or Fingernails

These work best on one major target area—the eyes. Using your fingers to rake, push, point, jab, or gouge an eye is a great defense.

Weapons That Don't Look Like Weapons

The beauty of self-defense is that practically any object you typically carry around in your purse, backpack, or pocket can be used as a weapon. The best part about these items is that they are an extension of your arm. In some situations, they can be used as an accompaniment to your strikes. Simply strike the target areas you learned about using the object as a driving force.

- **Books.** The corner of a book is a powerful weapon you can use to drive into the throat or the sinus cavity of an attacker.
- **Magazines.** Roll a magazine into a cylinder shape and use the bottom or top areas to drive into the attacker. Never swing it like a bat.
- **Wallets.** Use the edge of the wallet or the corner tips (in the same manner as the book) and strike your attacker in the throat or the eyes. This is particularly useful as an extension of your arm in executing a shuto strike; the edge of the wallet is used in the same manner as the fleshy side of your hand. You can also use the corner tips of the wallet to drive into the eyes.

- **Mobile phones.** Effective when used to strike any target areas on an attacker's body.
- **Pens, pencils, eyeliners, lip liners.** Best used when targeting the eye or the throat area.
- **Keys.** Drive keys into almost any target area.
- **Grocery or shopping bags.** If an attacker is coming toward you in a threatening manner, throw the bags directly into his face as a distraction. You can do the same thing with books or any other heavy object you are carrying in your hands or arms. It may buy you enough time to throw him off and run away.
- **Umbrellas.** If you are carrying a closed umbrella, you can open it up right in front of an attacker as a distraction to throw him off-guard, take away his vision, and run. You could also drive the sharp tip into an attacker's throat, temple, eyes, or other target area. Additionally, if the umbrella has a curved handle, you can use that curved part to wrap around the assailant's ankle, then pull back on the handle with the ankle inside the curved area to knock him to the ground.
- **Shoes.** If you are wearing high heels, you can use the heel portion of the shoe to stomp into the middle part of the attacker's foot. You can also take him to the ground by using the heel to hook around one of his ankles and push toward you, similar to one way you would use an umbrella.
- **Flashlights.** While I don't generally recommend using weapons in the place of physical self-defense, one piece of equipment out there is extremely beneficial for personal use. A company called SureFire makes personal flashlights; I particularly favor the one named Executive Defender, which has a light so strong and powerful, it temporarily blurs people's sight when it is flashed in their eyes.

Maximize Your Power

Torque Force

Don't worry; you don't need to spend ten hours a week lifting weights for this one. In the basic moves I detailed above, I have repeatedly given instructions to twist your wrist, hand, or what have you immediately before striking your target. Why? Torque, defined as a twisting force that provides extra horsepower, is what drives a strike. Torque motion catapults a strike forward immediately prior to impact so it releases the maximum amount of power at the point of impact. It's a similar motion to turning a doorknob to open the door, but not that large a movement. Using torque is a slight, subtle motion.

Try punching a still object, preferably something soft like a pillow, two different ways. First, punch with your fist hitting the target head-on, without using torque. Keep your wrist stationary as you throw the punch. Next, try throwing the same punch twisting your wrist very slightly (in a clockwise motion if you use your left hand, and counterclockwise if you use your right) just prior to impact. As you move your arm out, the twist will happen as the arm moves forward. Notice the difference? If you did it correctly, you'll actually feel more power driven from using the torque motion.

To use torque in a shuto strike, try this. Hold your hand in the shuto position (hand flat, fingers tightly together, thumb tucked against your palm) in front of your face so your palm is facing you. To execute the strike, twist your hand in a downward motion so that it ends up in a horizontal position, with your palm facing the floor. At the same time, your arm will bend in a ninety-degree angle. Using this twisting motion, strike your target. Then, without using torque, put your hand in a shuto strike position with your palm already facing the floor and strike your target. Your strike will not be as effective.

Using torque is all about focusing on the correct technique. Try practicing the basic strikes using this type of motion. At first, you'll need to consciously think about using torque, but after some time getting used to this motion, it will become natural to you.

Use Your Lower Body

Another way to maximize your power is by stepping into your defensive action. Upper-body movements (such as punches) are powered by your lower body. Lower-body movements (like kicks) are powered by your upper body. Instead of stepping forward to fuel a punch, step to the side or move your foot forward and then out to the side; this is also known as a fighting stance. If you were to step completely forward when striking, on the other hand, your leg distribution would be thrown off and your balance would not be level.

When you strike using your upper body, your power and strength begin in the bottom of your foot and flow upward through your entire body until they exit through your strike. When you strike an attacker, you must think of this starting power and imagine it moving through the lower part of your body into your upper body. Just like torque, you must practice this. You may not physically feel the power move through your body, but as you practice your strikes, make a conscious effort to think about the power moving up through your legs, through your buttock area, and through your strike. You will notice your lower-body muscles tensing as you strike. This is how it should feel, because your lower body is being put to use.

Strike and Pull Back Quickly

When you were a child, did anyone ever snap a towel over some part of your body? If so, you know how much it stings. Everyone knows that a towel is merely a piece of cloth that cannot cause any injury upon impact. Snapping a towel with rapid speed against a hard surface will cause pain, but most of the injury will come from having the towel snapped back as quickly after it hit its target.

When you strike an assailant, you want to attain the maximum power and strength out of that strike to weaken him. In itself, striking effectively is obviously critical; however, pulling back after striking is equally crucial. Don't let your hand, fist, or arm linger—even for a short amount of time—immediately after striking an assailant, or the hit will not yield its full debilitating effect. Try striking your thigh and allowing your hand to remain on your thigh for a second or two immediately after impact. Now try punching your thigh again; this time, pull your fist back immediately after striking. Feel the difference? When you let your hand linger after striking, the area that is hit automatically absorbs some of the impact of the strike. When you pull back, the injured area has no time to do anything except experience the full impact of the blow. The total effect of striking and pulling back quickly is what causes the greatest degree of injury and is what break bones.

Know When to Attack

Wait

What? That's right, wait. Usually, it is best to be patient and look for your opportunity to strike. The worst thing to do is to react too early or too quickly. You need to hold back on attacking until you know where the targets are that you can strike. As mentioned above, when attacked most people immediately respond by thrashing about and kicking and punching nothing but air. Self-defense is more of a waiting game than you think. Through the proper mental and physical training, it is possible for everything you learn to come into play so you can overcome this type of threatening situation.

Close the Gap

During an attack, it is natural to assume that the first thing you want to do is to get away from the attacker. Of course, if he hasn't grabbed on to you and you have the opportunity to run, go for it! But if you are in his grasp, it may be best to keep him as close to you as possible. Sound crazy?

It's not. Think of it this way. One of the self-defense techniques we will use is striking an attacker's eyes. (This may sound a tad grotesque, but when someone is trying to rape or murder you, believe me, you will not be thinking how disgusting striking his eyes can be. On the contrary, you will do anything to get the heck out of there.) Now, if an attacker's face is more than a few feet away, you will not have easy access to his eyes. If he is close to you, however, you can strike the eye, disable him, and run. If his torso is within striking distance, you can strike him in the pelvic area, another vulnerable spot.

You can't fight blind, and you can't defend yourself by striking something that is not within your reach. Either you need to close the gap by bringing yourself closer to him, or he will come toward you when he is feeling overly confident. Once he's close, you can strike and escape. Don't let distance stand between the attacker and you so that you cannot physically defend yourself. Close range is necessary to strike your targets. For example, if an assailant is a couple of yards away from you threatening you with a gun, hold your hands up in a surrender fashion, and let him know you don't want to be killed. As you speak, let him close the gap himself and move toward you to lessen the distance. Be sure never to make direct eye contact. Appear to be submissive, acting as if you will do whatever he says.

Common Distractions

Another opportunity for defense is when the attacker has ahold of you, but instead of assaulting you he launches into a one-sided conversation. Let's say he has you by the throat; his face and neck area will be in front of yours. He starts his violent monologue, voicing verbal threats and shouting expletives. While he may have your throat in his hands, your hands are free, and right in front of you are his throat and his face, which are yours for the taking. His talking is a distraction from the obvious scenario in front of your eyes—an exposed area that you can strike. The attacker's intention is to use his words to make you listen, and the more you listen, the more afraid you can become. You need to cut him off or tune him out.

If you see a vulnerable and exposed area on his body that you can strike, take it. Don't wait for him to stop talking and start assaulting.

Practice, Practice, Practice!

So what exactly are you practicing when it comes to self-defense? You are reinforcing your body's memory of how and where to strike. When you are learning the physical techniques while reading this book, you need to focus on getting the movements and the techniques executed properly. When I say *Strike with the edge of your hand, tucking in your thumb,* I mean exactly that, and that is how you should practice. The worst thing you can do for yourself is to practice the wrong technique. If you have painted anatomical parts on a punching bag, practice hitting the targets you intend to strike over and over again. If you aim for the eyes and strike the nose instead, keep repeating your actions until you consistently hit the eyes. Don't get frustrated if you don't hit your target dead-on each time; remember, consistency comes with practice.

The same thing applies to your physical technique. Throughout the chapters in this book, you are taught practical physical moves that you need to replicate with accuracy in learning self-defense. Exercise these moves at a slow pace so you can be sure you are doing everything correctly. If you are to pivot around but need to keep one of your legs still, practice doing that in the same exact way. Take your time; you only lose when you rush and perform the moves quickly but incorrectly.

Use a Friend

Most activities are more fun and exciting when you are sharing the experience with a partner. A lot of my clients tell me they are more motivated to work out when they are accompanied by one of their friends. Even something as boring as cleaning out the house can be a fun time if someone gives you a hand. You can share experiences and opinions, pointing out things that the other person is doing right or wrong. Use a friend to play criminal while you play potential victim; then switch roles. Put your self-defense moves to work! When you practice with a friend, your main objective is to enforce proper technique. Look at the position of the hand; watch for telegraphed body movements. And, of course, always be careful when striking.

Use Focus Pads

Martial artists and boxers often use relatively inexpensive leather and vinyl pads in their training. They look like boxing gloves, except focus pads have a flat surface and are used to develop accurate methods of striking. You'll need to have a friend aid you in this exercise. Have a friend put on these pads; you can practice striking on different points. You can also paint specific target points on them to develop accuracy. Additionally, you can practice the five basic strikes on the focus pads to get the techniques down pat.

Use a Punching Bag or Heavy Bag

You can use this accessory if you don't have a friend to practice with. Purchase a punching bag and mark anatomical parts on it. Draw the eyes, draw a throat, draw a pelvis, and practice striking these targets over and over so you become comfortable with where they are on a human body. Draw them in the same height where they normally would lie.

Visualize Attacks

Motivational speakers, professional athletes, politicians, life coaches, entrepreneurs and so on, all understand the importance of positive thinking and visualization in watching dreams come true. If you don't think you can do something, you can't. I've often read suggestions in books and magazines to imagine yourself where you want to be—create your dream of success, vision, wealth, and other good things. If you can visualize your dreams and step into subsequent action, you have created a window of opportunity for personal growth and success.

Can you visualize attacks? Can you picture yourself using the knowledge you've learned in this book and putting it to use? Can you picture yourself physically weakening a rapist and escaping his grip untouched? While you have learned useful information and hopefully understand the importance of practicing the physical aspect of self-defense, let your mind meet your body. Think about scary scenarios in your head and plan your getaway using the techniques in this book. Think about where you would strike and how you would strike. Think about the look of shock an attacker would display on his face when he realized he'd picked the wrong person as a victim. Visualize your victories. It's another way you can strengthen your confidence and prepare yourself in case you ever happen to be in a threatening environment.

Final Reminders

Before we get into the specific scenarios, there are a few more important elements to keep in mind when you execute physical self-defense moves. You have already been educated as to what, where, and how to strike. What else do you need to know?

Don't Telegraph Your Movement

The last thing you want to do is announce your moves. By that, I mean making them overly dramatic and executing them prematurely. You need to be smart in using what you know at the right time and not making a show of your knowledge until you're absolutely ready to follow through. The key in using the surprise tactic against your attacker is to make him believe you are defenseless and too afraid to defend yourself. You should begin a course of action only when you are ready to complete it.

By being overt in your defense, you risk two things happening. Number one, you risk your attacker noticing what you are trying to do—defend yourself. As a result, he may act more quickly to stop or de-escalate your actions. Number two, you risk missing opportunities to defend yourself. Say you're confronted by an attacker who is closing in on you. Rather than flailing about and striking blindly without a specific target in mind, wait until he comes near you. During that waiting process, which is really only a few seconds, don't rev up your arm in preparation for a strike. Don't raise your shoulder or move your hand such that he can see the beginning of your defenses. Keep your body still and calm your fears as much as possible. Wait until he is close and strike quickly. Strike with the minimum amount of movement possible.

Fight His Weaknesses, Not His Strengths

One of the most common concerns a woman has in using self-defense is her size. In physiological and hormonal fact, the average man is indeed bigger and stronger than the average woman. This fear, therefore, is somewhat valid. However, we need to remember what self-defense is: a method of protecting yourself, not a boxing or wrestling match. As I've said before, you are not fighting his brawn, you are striking his exposed target areas when he is least expecting it. You are fighting his weaknesses, not his strengths. Reminding yourself of this will help you recognize the power you can have over any attacker.

Run

If an attacker is a reasonably wide distance away from you, run. Remember, the best self-defense technique is the one you don't have to use. If there is an escape route, take it rather than waiting for the criminal to catch up with you. If you are being verbally threatened in a shopping center parking lot, run inside the store to get help. Anytime you have the opportunity to hightail it out of a possibly threatening situation, do so. You will not need to fight against someone who isn't there.

Don't Give Up

Criminals don't care who you are, where you come from, or what you stand to lose if you die or are raped. They only care about being stimulated by the power they have over you in an attack. You should already recognize the need for defense before an unfortunate situation ever occurs. Should you ever meet an attacker, weaken him, de-escalate his attack, and do whatever it takes to get out of there. Your life and the ones you love depend on it.

9

Sexual Assault and
Rape-Related Attacks

One of the greatest fears women hold is of being sexually assaulted or raped. It is a severely traumatic, humiliating, and demeaning crime that has, unfortunately, become so rampant that statistics now show that one in six women has been raped in her lifetime. While women are typically more vulnerable to rape than men, men can be victims just as well. This chapter will focus on female victims for simplicity's sake, but men can utilize these self-defense techniques as well; they work in the same manner, regardless of gender.

While sexual assaults and rapes can occur in multiple ways and in countless places, I'd like to share four typical scenarios experienced by female victims. While these stories are fictitious, such scenarios can happen. You will learn the specifics of each scenario and the self-defense techniques that can be used to stop or de-escalate an attack.

Windows of Opportunity

While every rape incident is unique, they do basically all share similar windows of self-defense opportunity. Think about it: When an attacker is attempting to rape you, you know his motive and you know what physically has to happen for the rape to be completed.

The primary windows of opportunity for physical defense in this situation are time and proximity.

Time

Get time on your side by (1) waiting for your attacker to come as close to you as possible so his target areas are right in front of you, and (2) waiting for him to be momentarily distracted when one or both of his hands are doing something. I know this may sound like a waiting game no one wants to play, but waiting is what can save your life. The trick is not to do anything until he's close or busy.

If your attacker has pinned your arms down, he'll have to free his grip at some point to complete the rape. Even if his hands are free, he will still have to be distracted at some point in time by doing whatever he logically needs to do to accomplish his task—for example, unclothe you, unbutton his pants, and so on. This is your moment. But be warned: This opportunity doesn't last long. It may be only a few seconds. If you immediately respond to the attack by panicking and flailing about, you might miss your chance.

You may be wondering what distractions an attacker will have if his intentions are to rape. They are so simple and obvious, they are easily overlooked.

- If you are in bed, he may have to pull the blankets or sheets off you to close in on your body.
- He may have to pull out a weapon—or he might be brandishing one. By holding on to or having to pull out his weapon, one of his hands will be busy, but the other hand will not.
- He will start to unclothe you or himself.

- He has to mount you or get on top of you somehow.
- If he wants to take you out of the house to rape you somewhere else, he's going to have to move both of you out of the house.

Proximity

Remember the importance of closing the gap. If an attacker is close to you, his target areas are also closer to you and you stand the greatest chance of striking them with accuracy and strength. In rape situations, proximity between an attacker and a victim is critical because the crime is intimately physical. This closeness isn't necessarily thought of as an advantage, for obvious reasons, and most victims in rape situations want the guy as far away as possible.

In theory this makes sense—a criminal who is not close to you will not hurt you. If he intends to harm you, however, he will move toward you. Remember that you are fighting his weaknesses, not his strengths, and because an attacker will usually physically overpower his victim, it is difficult to shove him off without incorporating some defensive techniques. These defensive tactics work best when he is close and he believes that you will not fight back.

Final Reminders

- Play the waiting game. Do not aimlessly throw your arms and legs around to keep an attacker away. Wait until he comes toward you. Once he is in your reach and distracted by something (such as un buckling his pants or unclothing you), strike him with your legs or your hands—whichever are closer and easiest to use.
- Remember the speed with which an attack and your subsequent defense happen. This is all accomplished in a matter of a few seconds.

Because an attack happens so fast, your reaction needs to be just as fast.

- These techniques are interchangeable. Go for whatever target on the attacker's body is the closest and easiest to strike. Use more than one technique to debilitate your attacker and acquire as much time as possible to run away and get help.

- You absolutely must not worry about him chasing after you subsequent to you striking him. Your main concern is to strike him as hard as possible to weaken him so he cannot run after you. Use this time to run and get help immediately.

- Practice, practice, practice! You need to review these moves mentally and physically so they become second nature to you. The last thing you want to do is read through these techniques, forget about them, and have no clue what a shuto strike is three weeks from now. Take a few minutes every couple of days and practice striking. Practice feeling your throat area for target areas. Get used to where the target zones are on a body. Practicing will pay off should you ever be in an unfortunate situation and need to use these techniques.

Sexual Assault Scenario #1:
Stranger in the House

You live alone in a first-floor luxury apartment in a suburban American town. Although you have never considered yourself a potential victim of crime, you are diligent in locking your doors and windows and pay considerable attention to your surroundings and persons exhibiting suspicious behavior. On this particular night, nothing out of the ordinary occurs and you proceed with your routine of checking all doors and windows prior to going to bed. All is quiet and all is safe.

In the middle of the night, you are startled by strange noises near your bedroom door and see the shadow of a man on the wall opposite your bed. You are petrified and begin to panic. "Who's out there," you yell, frozen to your bedsheets by fear.

The shadow disintegrates and now you can clearly see a tall, rather hefty man dressed in black moving toward your bed. As you frantically fumble to grab the phone on your nightstand, he starts warning you not to scream. He moves closer to you and starts climbing onto the bed, continuing to talk in a threatening fashion. He tears the bedsheet off you and starts to pin your arms back over your head with his hands.

What do you do?

Self-Defense Techniques

The first thing to remember is to stay calm and not panic. This may sound unreasonable, and to a certain extent it's almost impossible. However, being calm might save your life and give you time to think; being hysterical will not.

Ignore his verbal threats and mentally block out any conversation he tries to make. His one-sided dialogue is solely a method of intimidation. The more he drones on and on, the more he knows you will listen, and your level of fear will be heightened. If you talk back in desperate pleas begging him to stop or leave, you will become more panicked. Don't allow his method of intimidation to negatively influence your reaction.

Let the scenario build to the point where he is close to you. The attacker needs to be convinced you will not fight back—that you are paralyzed by fear. This will make him confident and subsequently vulnerable, because his arrogance will ultimately lead to a lack of awareness. He is apt to become sloppy.

I will introduce two methods of self-defense techniques for this scenario.

If you can gain the use of your hands and arms, there are several options you can use in self-defense. As the attacker is drawing near to you, it is likely that his face and neck will be right in front of yours. This gives you an easy target—strike anywhere debilitating on the entire face or throat:

- If you decide to take his eyes, take one or both of your thumbs and drive them right through his eyes.
- If you decide to strike the throat, you can use either a shuto strike (the flat-hand move) or use the web of your hand. If you use the shuto strike, don't forget to tuck in your thumb to make sure your hand is as rigid as possible. Strike the throat with your hand in a horizontal position, parallel to the ground. If your other hand is free, you can reinforce your strike by using it to push your striking hand forward. As you move to strike the throat with your horizontal hand—let's say it's your right hand—take your left hand and use the palm to vertically strike your horizontal, right-hand strike. If you use the web of your hand, strike his throat, crushing his windpipe.
- If you have both hands free, you can cup your attacker's ears and quickly clap your hands against them to blow out his eardrums.
- As soon as you have disabled him, run and get help.

If you recall Caryn's story in the first chapter, she used her calm composure and her legs as weapons. This bought her the time she needed to escape and can be an option for you as well. As your attacker draws near to you and is getting on top of you, he will need to undo his pants or adjust his clothing in order to fulfill the rape. This is your greatest window of opportunity. As his body approaches and while you are remaining calm, do the following:

- Draw your knees and push out with your feet, slamming the flats of both feet into his chest or pelvic region. Use as much upper-body strength as possible to power this kick. Remember, your upper body fuels lower-body actions.

• Run and get help. Don't stop and think about the possibility of him chasing you. Your number one priority is getting away, and you've found your chance.

Sexual Assault Scenario #2:
A Date Gets Out of Hand

You are on a date with your co-worker Joe. He seems like a reasonably nice guy; he's smart, funny, and good looking. During dinner, you notice he somewhat forcibly tries to grab your hand on several occasions, though in what you consider a playful and flirty fashion. Your conversation seems harmless enough, so you don't worry about his actions. You leave the restaurant and Joe offers to drive you home. Although you live only a few blocks away and it seems a perfect night for a stroll, you accept his offer.

During the drive, Joe begins to act a little more aggressively, and you start to feel very uncomfortable. He makes more than one sexually inappropriate comment and tries to put his hand on your thigh. Because he is a co-worker, you find the situation more and more awkward. While you are not welcoming his advances by any means, for some reason he is not getting the message. You are unsure of how to be more straightforward in communicating your discomfort about his behavior.

You stop in front of your house, and Joe puts the car in park. You turn to him and politely thank him for dinner, remarking on what a lovely time you had. Joe leans in to kiss you, but you swing your head slightly away so he misses your mouth. You notice how angry he is starting to become. "No, Joe," you say, "I'll see you at work tomorrow." As you open the car door to get out, Joe realizes he is not getting anywhere with you.

Before you can get out, he grabs your shirt collar and pulls you back into the vehicle. "What are you doing?" you yell. He drives off toward a parking area far enough away that passersby can't see or hear what's happening inside the car, and tries to rape you.

What do you do?

Self-Defense Techniques

As always, stay calm. A man attacking the way Joe did will fall into the power assertive category of rapists. He's violent, he's physically and verbally aggressive, and he gets a kick out of intimidating and humiliating women.

Most likely, he will keep you in the car and come over the console. He might attempt to get you into the backseat of the vehicle to rape you, but that would mean getting you out of the automobile in a public environment, and may draw attention he doesn't want. The last thing he wants is to get caught.

If he has you in a secure position in the passenger seat and starts to mount you, you can do a few things:

- If the seat is not yet in a horizontal position, you can surprise him by hitting the lever located on the side (closest to the door) of the passenger seat. This will knock him off-balance, and he will automatically fall on top of you. His initial leverage in the situation was being in control on top of you, but if he is thrown on top of you without that control, this leverage automatically disappears. The worst problem in this case is that his body weight is directly on top of yours, but nothing bad can come out of it. He can't rape you like that, can he? And because his face will be close to yours, your best target is the throat or the eyes. Here is your opportunity.

- Expose his throat area so you can strike it. Use the palm of your hand and force his chin up. This force will push his head back, leaving his throat available for your defensive strike.
- You can grab his throat and squeeze, collapsing his trachea (windpipe), or use the shuto technique to the throat.

All these self-defense techniques will work to severely weaken his advances enough so you can throw him off you, get out of the car, and run. Because your space is limited in this type of situation, it is crucial to strike as hard as you can and with the most accuracy. This way, throwing him off you is easier because he is severely injured. You could also use two different techniques together (gouging the eyes and striking the throat, for instance) to weaken him to the fullest extent possible.

Sexual Assault Scenario #3:
Working Late

You are working late in a high-rise office building. It's almost eight o'clock on a Friday night, and most people have left the building to go home or to happy hour. You just want to get a couple of things finished in anticipation of a mini vacation you will be taking the following week. After all, holidays away from work are always better when you know all your projects have been completed prior to your hiatus.

You cross the last thing off your "to do" list and begin to shut down your computer. Stifling a yawn as you gather up your belongings, your mind starts to wander. You have worked a straight nine-hour day and fatigue is beginning to kick in. You sling your pocketbook over your shoulder, lock up your office space, and head down the long corridor to get to the elevator. At some point, you think you hear footsteps, but you don't pay much attention—at least not enough to make you stop and look around. You take out your cell phone, which was in your coat pocket, and keep it in your hand, just in case.

You reach the elevator and press the DOWN key. Waiting impatiently, you stare straight ahead at the elevator doors. You want to get out of there as quickly as possible and go home. The elevator chimes, announcing its arrival on your floor, and you walk right in. As the doors are about to close, a man walks into the elevator and stands near the button pad. As soon as the elevator doors close and it starts to descend, he slams his fist on the STOP button. The elevator jolts and subsequently stands still in between two floors. The man moves in front of you in an intimidating fashion, his face two inches away from yours, and says, "Now I have you all to myself."

What do you do?

Self-Defense Techniques

Pay attention! Remember that you are most vulnerable when you are in your own world. This is especially critical when you're walking in an unpopulated area, such as an empty parking lot or, in this case, an empty office building late at night. If you're waiting for something or someone alone, whether you're near an elevator or waiting for a bus or train, don't look straight ahead. Look around, or stand sideways so you have peripheral vision and can see what's happening on all sides. Be aware of your surroundings. If you think you hear footsteps, don't brush it off. Look around; notice what is happening around you so are better prepared.

Because you are carrying your cell phone, you can use that for self-defense. Here is what you can do.

- Did you know that because the assailant is standing so close to you, you just entered into a zone where his weakness is directly in front of you? What is it? He is so close to you, his target areas are open for striking. The gap has been closed, and he has done it himself.

- As he threatens you and invades your space, use the time to play actress. Put your hands up in surrender and tell him you don't want to get hurt; you'll just do whatever he says. He'll probably assume you are as weak and unaware as he expected.
- Then strike his chin back with the heel of your palm. This will push his head back and expose his throat area even more.
- Strike his throat with your cell phone. You can also strike his temples. If you choose to use your hands, strike his eyes or his pelvic area. Because the elevator is stopped, you need to completely debilitate him so he will not get up. Striking the target areas mentioned, especially the throat, will do this.
- Once he is down, hit the STOP button again to release the elevator and hit the EMERGENCY button as well so the entire building will be alerted. Get out on any floor, run, and get help. Use your cell phone to call others, too, and alert them to the situation.

Sexual Assault Scenario #4:
Date Rape

"Would you like to come in, John? We can watch the tail end of *CSI*." Normally, you would never invite a guy into your home on the second date, but John is such a sweetheart. He makes you laugh, he's incredibly intelligent, and he has such a way with people with his Southern charm. You never thought you could actually meet someone with so much potential on an Internet dating service! During dinner, the waitress practically fell in love with him because he treated her like a friend, not some random person working in the service industry.

"Sure, I'd love it," he replies. "As long as you're okay with it." *What a nice guy*, you think.

As both of you head into the living room, you take his jacket, put it on one of the kitchen chairs, and start to make a fresh pot of gourmet coffee. John plops himself down on the living room couch and turns on the TV. "Hey, coffee smells delicious," he yells from across the room.

When you return with two piping hot mugs, you both get comfortable on the couch. You are sitting very close together and the mood is incredibly romantic. You opted not to watch *CSI*, choosing a random movie with a very young Richard Gere. John starts to rub your thigh and you engage in a nice, sweet kiss. While his kiss seems gentle, you notice that the pressure from his hands has strangely increased. It makes you nervous, but you brush the feeling off.

After a few moments, he starts to move his hands in places you'd just rather not be touched. He starts to whisper in your ear how sexy and beautiful you are. You get a bad feeling in the pit of your stomach and start to say, "No, not yet, John." This guy doesn't stop. He continues to kiss your neck.

What do you do?

Self-Defense Techniques

This is a situation where you need to immediately heed your gut instinct and stop the situation before it begins to escalate. You have to be continuously aware of what your intuition is telling you. One of its jobs is to help you recognize some red-flag behavior in other people and places so you can determine whether or not you should remove yourself from the situation. If a date is starting to make you uncomfortable, give yourself the permission to acknowledge that feeling as truth and do something about it. Specifically, get out of there. If you are in your house, you are in a location where you have the space to immediately run away. If you refer back to the attempted rape in the vehicle, you didn't have an opportunity to initially run; you had to physically weaken your assailant first. In your house, however, you have the space and know an immediate exit route to leave.

If a guy doesn't listen to you the first time you say no, while you don't necessarily have to gouge his eye out, you can shove him off and get out of there. Chances are, if it's a date, he won't immediately leap on top of you and start to unbutton his pants; he will instead let the momentum increase and then move in. You need to leave before he gets that chance. Push him away, call a friend, or run out of the house to a neighbor's.

If you are in your house and he doesn't leave, then you leave your house. Trust me, he doesn't want to look like a bad guy standing in someone else's house as a guest after the host has left. His reputation will be marred that way.

Do whatever it takes for you to feel safe. That is the most important rule of thumb.

Although we often feel safe in or near a motor vehicle, we're not—despite the strength and security of its steel construction and locked doors. Can you use a car to your advantage? Will it serve as a stationary hindrance? How can you defend yourself when you are trapped in your vehicle and have few or no opportunities for movement?

Believe me, there are things you can do. Let's find out.

Motor Vehicle Scenario #1:
Road Rage

It is an early Saturday morning . . . well, early enough for you on a day you have the option of sleeping in past seven o'clock. While last night's poker game with the guys was like any other ordinary Friday night, you managed to leave the festivities as the winner of five hundred bucks. Not too shabby for a guy who just learned the basics of Texas Hold 'Em only a few weeks ago, you think. And now, on this early morning, you are off to Wal-Mart to stock up on hunting supplies; after all, deer season opens in a few days.

You hop in your pickup truck, grateful that the giant superstore is only a couple of miles away. While you'd swap suburban life for a cabin in the woods any day, the convenience of being able to purchase basically anything—from groceries to tennis shoes to jewelry for your girlfriend—is definitely a perk. You pull out of your driveway and start heading toward Wal-Mart, thinking of nothing other than binoculars, camouflage parkas, and top-of-the-line tree stands.

Right before the stoplight where you'd have to make a right to drive into the enormous parking lot, you realize your daydreaming has caused you to stay in the middle lane; unless you get over to the right lane immediately, you'll miss your turn. You jolt to attention, and without putting your turn signal on you swiftly maneuver your pickup truck into the right lane to catch your turn. You don't realize you just cut off a driver who's had a very bad morning.

You are alarmed to hear a blaring horn and muted shouts. As you drive into the parking lot, you glance into your rearview mirror and see an irate man in a fancy sports car behind you giving you the finger and ranting and raving like a maniac. You raise your hand in the mirror to express your apologies and simultaneously mouth the words *I'm sorry* to him. He continues to honk his car horn and yell a monologue of rage and expletives. While you are deeply apologetic, now you are also somewhat worried. Driving into a parking space, you roll down your window and say, "Hey man, I'm sorry; I didn't see where I was going. I didn't mean to cut you off." You start getting out and notice the man just parked his car perpendicular to your truck and is storming toward you.

"What do you think you're doing, you mother—" Before you have a chance to respond, he has grabbed you by the shoulders and slams you against your own truck.

What do you do?

Self-Defense Techniques

Road rage is scary to think about. While most of us would define ourselves as typically good drivers, there are times where we do get distracted, whether by our thoughts, our screaming kids in the car, or figuring out where we are if we're lost. And when that happens, sometimes we do drive through the light that just turned red . . . or make sharp turns without notice . . . or even cut other drivers off. We have no clue as to what the reaction of the driver we've innocently slighted will be. Hopefully, he will be understanding and let our mistake go. But sometimes people don't know how to do that.

In this scenario, the man who was headed to Wal-Mart got out of his vehicle before he was assaulted by the angry driver. If you ever find yourself in a similar situation and have the opportunity to stay inside your car, do so, and start beeping your horn furiously. Honking will draw attention to the situation and alarm the assailant. You are safer remaining inside your car or truck than confronting the individual with apologies. Stay in the car, honk the horn, make a lot of noise, and, if you have a cell phone, call someone—a friend, a family member, or local authorities.

Now, because this man has already gotten out of his car and been slammed against his truck, he has no choice but to employ self-defense techniques. Here is what you can do in such a situation:

- The assailant's arms are near your shoulder area, so in order to strike a target, you need to force his arms out of the way to expose his head and neck area. Take your hands underneath his arms and strike his arms apart.
- Now that his upper body is exposed, you can cup your hands over his ears and slam them with full force, strike his throat in a shuto strike, or even strike his eyes.

- You can finish the move by stomping on the middle part of his foot with the heel of your shoe to break the bones.

Additionally, you'll notice that the attacker boxed in the victim's car; if this driver had remained inside his vehicle, he wouldn't have been able to back up and exit the parking lot. If you are ever boxed in similarly, have no escape route, and are confronted by a visibly angry person who starts to violently bang on your car, stay in your vehicle. If you have a cell phone, call the authorities. If the person will not let up and you fear for your life, start backing up into his car. Keep driving in reverse and hitting his car until you can escape. Remember, the rule of thumb is never to abandon your vehicle. You are always safer inside than outside facing the wrath of a raging driver.

Motor Vehicle Scenario #2:
Rear-End Collision

You are driving on a local highway with two of your closest girlfriends, Brianna and Jennifer. They both flew into town this morning for your ten-year high school reunion. The three of you have spent the entire day in nostalgic reflections on the past and marveling over where each of you has ended up in her life.

"Remember the prom and your little drama with Nick the Slick?" Brianna recalls. You and Jennifer burst out laughing and you shake your head in remembrance. Boy, you were the most insecure teenager alive and everything exploded on prom night, when you became insanely jealous after seeing your date embrace one of his friends, who happened to be a girl.

"Yeah," you laugh in response. "And can you believe he actually married me? Here Nick and I are, two kids later!"

All three of you continue giggling. Jennifer puts in a CD she compiled with all the favorite songs you enjoyed listening to way back when. The three of you dance in your seats to the rhythm of "You're Unbelievable" and are completely oblivious to the huge pickup truck storming down the highway a couple of yards behind you.

"Remember when—" Brianna is cut off when your vehicle is tapped from behind by that pickup. All three of you bolt slightly forward, but thankfully you are wearing seat belts. *What a pain,* you think, *a rear-end collision.*

What do you do?

Self-Defense Techniques

While this scenario was not necessarily provoked by an actual attacker in a typical sense, I chose to include it because I get asked about it quite frequently. While getting rear-ended by another vehicle seems like an innocent and negligent mistake, you can't be sure. Being safe in today's world means taking appropriate precautions.

When I redirect this scenario back to the person asking about it, I generally get this response: "I would stop the car and get out . . ." to assess the damage, talk to the other driver, and so on. My first rule of thumb is never to abandon your vehicle. If you get rear-ended, don't automatically assume the other driver hit your car by accident and, consequently, exit your vehicle to communicate. Stay in your car instead.

Before you take any course of action, call someone. In this day and age, almost everybody carries their cell phones around with them. Call a friend or a relative and note exactly what happened, when it happened, where you are, and, if possible, information about the other vehicle and driver who hit you.

If you are hit from behind, you need to establish whether it was an accident or someone slammed into you on purpose. Typically, criminals will not slam into your car with extreme force—that will automatically raise your suspicions. They will be subtle and tap your car gently in the manner of an innocent rear-end collision.

If you are hit from behind, first put on your hazard lights to let the other driver know you are responding to the accident. Proceed to drive into a lighted and populated area—a gas station, a shopping center, a grocery store. If you were hit by accident, the person will likely follow you to apologize, exchange information, and assess damages to both vehicles. If the other driver follows you and you get out of your car in a populated area, you have increased your level of safety. No true criminal wants to get caught, so if he happens not to be legit, chances are he won't attack you in this type of environment. If someone hits you from behind with a full intent to harass or harm you, he will not follow you to a populated area and will likely drive off. Remember, criminals don't want to be caught. And to a criminal, where there's light and a lot of people around, it means the presence of witnesses and an environment where he will be seen, heard, and, if he proceeds to attack, ultimately caught.

Motor Vehicle Scenario #3:
The Mall Parking Lot

The "to do" list has grown. Go to the grocery store. Check. Go to the dry cleaners. Check. Find and purchase book for your son's elementary school graduation gift. Check. Go to the mall and get new outfits for yourself and your baby daughter. Check. You leave the mall and breathe a welcome sigh of relief. Your baby coos with delight in the stroller that your right hand is maneuvering with absolute dexterity.

The baby starts to whine and reminds you feeding time is fast approaching, and you need to pick up your son from school in half an hour. You smile and, once you spot your minivan, are grateful you found a somewhat close parking space. You don't notice the unmarked white van to the right of yours, but the stranger inside has a perfect view of you and your toddler. He watched you pull into the parking space an hour and a half ago and decided you were his perfect prey. He knew you would return to your vehicle distracted by the shopping bags, by the baby in the stroller, by trying to find car keys.

While he waits, you toss the bags into the backseat of the van and begin to unbuckle the stroller straps so you can secure your child into her car seat. Little Amy is now squirming in your arms, eyes aglow from your tender touch and smile. *She makes it all worth it,* you think as she lets out a laugh. You put your daughter in her car seat, double-checking the straps for security, and look toward the stroller. You don't notice the engine being started in the white van. You don't see the man inching his way toward the sliding door, ducking his head from its windows, though they're tinted anyway. He is smiling. You are smiling. For different reasons.

Your finger is about to hit the RELEASE button on the stroller when you hear the sliding door on the van parked beside you. In a matter of seconds, you become attuned to some movement, but as your neck swings around to determine the cause of commotion, it's too late. He has grabbed you with one hand on the back of your hair and the other covering your mouth.

What do you do?

Self-Defense Techniques

Remember to pay attention, especially in parking areas. Vans are the easiest type of vehicle to use for abducting victims. Number one, the height and length of a van matches or is greater than that of an average car. It prevents you from seeing what is happening around you, as well as preventing other people from seeing what's happening where you are. Number two, van abductions are as simple as sliding a door open, grabbing someone, pushing her in the vehicle, and sliding the door shut. It happens so fast and so easily.

If you see a van parked next to your vehicle, don't be afraid or embarrassed to have someone walk you to your car. You can also be proactive and offensive in your actions. Look through the windows of the van, or, if they're tinted, look through the windshield. When you are alert, aware, and engage in proactive behavior, you are usually immediately disqualified as an easy target. And that is exactly what you want to have happen.

If you are grabbed from behind, as in the scenario above, here's what to do.

- One of my favorite techniques for attacks from behind is to turn right around and into your attacker and, essentially, close the gap. Figure out which way your body can move. If you can't move to the left, you should be able to move to the right, and vice versa. After deciding on the direction to move, put your weight on the opposite leg. Take your other leg and step sideways over his foot (your right foot would step over his right foot, or your left foot would step over his left). Turn your upper body toward him.
- Immediately after turning around to face him, strike his pelvis with the heel of your hand. Remember to pull back immediately after striking. If you have easy access to his throat or eyes, take those as well.
- Now that you have weakened him, you can also sweep him off his feet as discussed under Going Low in chapter 8. Turn all the way around and drop down to the ground so your head is facing his lower body. Use the inside (palm area) of your hands and place them on the inside of his ankles. Pull his ankles toward you and watch him go down.
- Now grab your baby, run or drive away, and get help!

Motor Vehicle Scenario #4:
Car Trouble

You are driving down back roads to avoid the traffic on Interstate 40 so you can make your parents' thirtieth wedding anniversary dinner on time. You are in charge of meeting and greeting the guests, so this is one event you can't afford to be late to. You think you hear something funny, then realize you do—bumping and flapping noises. You have a flat tire.

"Oh crap," you curse as you slam your hands against your steering wheel. You carefully steer your Jeep to the side of the road and get out. You are less than a quarter mile away from the main road where your parents live, so if you change the flat fast enough, tardiness shouldn't be an issue. You open the back door of your Jeep and start collecting the spare tire, tire iron, and jack from the back compartment. You glance up at the dark sky and are amazed to see a plethora of stars dotting the horizon . . . something you've never taken the time to notice before. In that instant, you seem to hear a car coming down the road a mile or so away. *Maybe someone else knows this shortcut*, you think.

As you start to raise your Jeep with the jack, you can definitely hear sounds of a car approaching. Once you have gotten the spare on, you see a car pulling over toward you and someone getting out.

"Hey there," the stranger yells. "Is everything okay? Do you need some help?"

"No, I'm fine," you respond. "I'm just changing a flat and I'll be done in a second. Thanks, sir."

The man moves closer toward you. "Hey, it's no problem, I can help you, I do it all the time."

You start getting suspicious. "No, I'm okay. I'm fine. No problem here, buddy."

The man is now a few feet away from you, and as he moves closer he subtly draws something out of his pocket. It's too dark to see it clearly, but you catch sight of a glint of metal—it's either a knife or a gun.

What do you do?

Self-Defense Techniques

As a stranded roadside driver, you need to employ extra caution. I generally advise my students never to accept help from strangers; there have been too many accounts of false Good Samaritans and murdered roadside victims. This especially applies if you are by yourself. If someone pulls over to assist, tell him that you have already called AAA, the police, a friend, or a family member, and folks are on their way to help. In this instance, there were weapons around that the driver could have used. Here is what you could do.

- As soon as the stranger is walking toward you, pick up the tire iron—or any grippable object that would stick out of your fist—just in case the situation escalates. You hide the weapon by placing the part that is sticking out toward you, so the person cannot see it.
- If he approaches you in a life-threatening manner, use the tire iron as an extension of your arm and strike his throat, sternum, or pelvis. Don't swing it around aimlessly; use it to strike a specific target in the same manner as you would use your hands to strike. You can basically use this weapon to strike any target area that would debilitate the attacker.
- Run and get help. If you have a cell phone, call someone. If you can get into your car and drive off, do so, even if it means driving on a flat tire. If you can run to a place of business or a residence, do that.

11

When There's
More than One

Famous martial artists in Hollywood movies have no trouble being confronted by multiple attackers. Neither did Neo in the *Matrix* sequel when he fought against numerous replicas of Agent Smith. It looks almost easy on screen. The so-called victim of numerous opponents moves with agility and grace; the attackers seem to pause in their fighting sequence so the victim has enough time to react effectively. You could even call it art.

Unfortunately, we all know that life is not Hollywood. Not even close. Being faced with two or more criminals is certainly a challenge. It might seem like an opportunity to admit immediate defeat. However, should this ever happen to you, you need to remember that initially setting yourself up for failure means you will fail. You have not even given yourself a chance. Telling you this is nothing new, I understand, but in this type of situation understanding and using your knowledge is critical. Having a solid mental attitude of strength, hope, and perseverance is especially important in a multiple-attacker scenario because it's such an intimidating challenge.

Pick One—the Mouth or the Closest

One of the most important strategies to use when you are in the middle of being attacked in this manner is to choose one guy to fight. You can't fight them all; this is not Hollywood or a martial arts movie. It is definitely feasible for experts trained in combating multiple assailants to have a significantly high chance of survival in fighting all of them. Most people, unfortunately, are not trained experts. The fancy and complicated moves you see carried out by professionals do not work so well when enacted by the average human being. Therefore, keep your self-defense techniques as simple as possible. Focus on one person and make him your escape. You need to do this to create a distraction and get you the time you need to run away.

So which one do you choose? In a group attack, there is generally a leader in the pack. I refer to this individual as the "mouth." He is the talker, the challenger, the intimidator, and the one whom almost everyone follows. He is hard to miss and ignore. He is the loudest of the bunch, the most arrogant, and the most demanding.

The mouth is the core strength of the group and the best person to attack first, if possible. Taking this guy out will eliminate the backbone of the group of attackers. This gives you more of a chance to flee as fast as you can.

If it's not physically advantageous to strike the mouth of the group from where you are, the next person to choose is the one who is closest to you. Taking that guy will give you the opportunity and time to escape. You can use most of the physical strategies I have mentioned thus far to create your defenses.

Regardless of whom you decide to strike first, the thing to remember is to strike hard and strike fast. Additionally, after deciding on who, you need to close the gap in order to strike. Always be subtle when you do this.

Don't be overt in your moves; don't telegraph your actions. Always play the actor and pretend that you are submissive, scared, and will do whatever they say. Take one of these two assailants out and run. Use your mental fortitude to fuel your physical actions and believe you can escape.

Use Your Environment to Your Advantage

Where are you? When you are attacked by more than one person, assessing your environment is a necessity. This is not complicated nor time consuming. Think of where you are standing. Is it a closed space or a large one? Is there enough room to run, or are you trapped in a tight area? If you are in the type of environment where you can reasonably escape, do so. If not, you have no choice but to use physical self-defense.

Additionally, if your environment is in a setting where there are houses or open places of businesses, use them to your advantage. Run into a house or a store or a populated area. Yell, scream, and create commotion to draw public attention and distract the attackers from pursuing and completing their intended assault.

Use whatever you have around you—whether that's houses or extra space—to your advantage to increase your chances of survival.

What You See Is What You Get

When there are two or more assailants in the line of attack, your ability to see peripherally is crucial. To focus on only one attacker means that you don't know where the others are or what they're doing. You need to pay attention to what's going on around you so you can effectively strike and run away. Here are two important things to remember:

- **Look peripherally.** Don't make eye contact with the person who is closest to you. All that does is limit your vision. You need to be able to see all around you. Don't focus your eyes on one object or person for too long. Instead look around periodically in all directions.
- **Never give them your body.** You never want to be positioned directly in front of your attacker. You should stand sideways instead of being face-to-face. Doing this will weaken his ability to strike a direct target on your body. In addition, when you incorporate a sideways stance, your peripheral vision is increased. Lastly, if you can find a stationary object that you can push your back against, such as a car or a telephone pole, use it. It is always better to be against something and have all your attackers in your front view, rather than have them surrounding you.

Multiple Attacker Scenario #1:
On Campus

Nine harmonious gongs echo throughout campus from the newly built bell tower. It's enough time to head back home and change outfits before your boyfriend's fraternity party. You quicken your pace as you swing your backpack with your right arm, securing its position on your back.

You never were that comfortable taking the back roads to get to your campus apartment. But it wasn't quite an issue of safety; it was those haunting reminders from your parents to stay on main roads. You can almost hear them now, chiding you and shaking their heads in disappointment. "Mary," your mother would say, "if I've told you once, I've told you a billion times, saving a few minutes of your time is not worth putting your safety at risk." You roll your eyes, thankful that you live three hundred miles away from your overly protective parents. I mean, for goodness' sake, they didn't let you date until you were eighteen, they enforced a strict midnight curfew on weekends, and you had to practically beg and plead to get them to let you attend a university in another state. They would totally freak out if they knew you had a boyfriend. And a senior who belonged to a fraternity, for that matter!

Your fingers protectively curl around two chemistry books and a lab notebook. It is such an inconvenience to be holding them, but your backpack is already full with what feels like six thousand books and notepads. As you continue walking through the brownstone-lined streets, you notice the uniqueness, charm, and coziness of each building. They could almost pass for houses, except the ENGLISH DEPARTMENT and FUNDAMENTAL LITERATURE signs are dead giveaways.

A few hundred feet away, you see the shadows of two young men walking toward you. As you move closer toward them, their rambunctious behavior starts to grow louder and stronger. They look drunk or high or something. One of the guys starts yelling out some catcalls with obviously slurred speech, and his compadre joins in on the fun. You roll your eyes. They look to be wearing university athletic sweatshirts, so they have to be a couple of drunken frat brothers.

"Where ya goin', baby," the louder man calls out.

You move to the opposite sidewalk and walk faster. They make a dash to follow you on the other side of the street and begin to circle you.

"Hey! Hey, wha's your name?" One of the guys moves closer to you and reaches his hand out to stroke your cheek, then grabs you by the shirt.

What do you do?

Self-Defense Techniques

If you are walking in this type of public environment and start to get harassed by multiple belligerent persons, move toward a car, a house, or a random person nearby. As you go, pretend that you know exactly where you're going and whom you are walking toward. Criminals are more likely to attack folks who either look lost or look like they have a long way to walk toward their destination.

If this is not possible and the attackers are already starting to circle you in close proximity, limiting your ability to escape, you need to move into attack mode. Now you are forced to deal with the attackers and have to pick one to strike—the mouth or the one physically closest to you.

- Lift your hands up in surrender fashion and tell them that you don't want to get hurt. Act as if you are scared and completely willing to comply with their demands. Remember not to make eye contact with any of the attackers. Be subtle in your efforts to stand sideways and not directly in front of your attackers. Maintain the greatest possible amount of peripheral vision without telegraphing your sideway movement. It is enough if you just turn slightly so your body is not an open target. If there is something that you can put your back against to keep these guys right in front of you, take it. You never want to be surrounded if you can help it.
- As you stand with your hands raised, slowly move toward the attacker you have chosen to strike. Close the gap.
- Strike the eyes or the throat to weaken him.

Multiple-Attacker Scenario #2:
An Unfamiliar Neighborhood

You finally got it! The last missing arcade game for the collection you have spent the past eight years researching and accumulating for your game room at home. It's a vintage Pac-Man arcade game in almost perfect condition . . . and for a price that was impossible to beat! Your wife thinks you're crazy for driving three hours away from home to pick it up from the eBay seller, but you know the long drive is totally worth it. It's practically priceless because you understand how much value there really is in finding that one missing collector's piece. Pac-Man. You start to think about the yellow bleeping object and its colorful ghostly enemies chomping on white dots and chasing each other through the maze patterns. God, you could play Pac-Man for hours.

As you drive along Highway 73, you dial into a radio station playing 1980s music. It makes you even more excited to load the game onto the pickup truck you borrowed from your best friend, Matt. And it even makes you a little nostalgic. Suddenly, you realize you should be concentrating on figuring out where you are exactly.

The directions to this man's house lie on top of the console. *Take exit 33 off Highway 73 and bear right off the ramp* is the next direction scrawled in your awful handwriting. You continue to follow the directions exactly as marked and find yourself driving down the main road of a dilapidated neighborhood. *This is odd*, you think. There is a long stretch of houses that would seem abandoned if not for the plethora of children's toys strewn in the yards and the multiple cars parked in each driveway. Dingy shutters dangle awkwardly under the windows of the houses you pass, and screen doors are either torn off their frame or have holes punched in them. There are a few people milling around the front porches in some of the houses, but otherwise the area seems generally empty. It feels like an episode out of *The Twilight Zone*.

This can't be right; you must have written the directions wrong. You maneuver your vehicle to make a U-turn in one of the driveways and start heading in the opposite direction toward Highway 73. As you drive, you notice a group of men and women walking in the middle of the street toward your SUV. As you get closer to them, you notice they start to form a human chain, walking shoulder-to-shoulder, and it doesn't appear that they are slowing down. *Is this a gang?* you wonder. *Where the hell am I?*

You continue to drive toward them, but they don't get out of your way. What do you do?

Self-Defense Techniques

My suggestion is not going to be entirely self-defense-related, because you will not be confronting this crowd directly, and you won't use your body in defense. I recommend staying in your vehicle. When you are in any type of automobile-related attack, don't get out of your car. It is your main source of protection.

Keep driving down the road. If the group doesn't budge out of your path of travel, keep driving. You may balk at this suggestion, but think about it. The people clearly have no respect for your boundaries; they are agitated and are likely to be exhibiting violent behavior. The ones who don't want to get hit by an oncoming car will move out of the way. The others simply have a death wish.

Multiple-Attacker Scenario #3:
Sunset at the Beach

God, it's great living right on the beach, you think as you stretch your legs out over your towel and sink your toes into the cool sand. The salty smell of the ocean wafts through the air and stimulates your senses, and you experience the peculiar combination of feeling simultaneously energized yet completely relaxed. Staring into the setting sun, you wonder why you don't come out to see this picturesque view more often. There are a few other people out there besides you. You see a man and woman jogging on the shoreline, a man taking photographs of the sunset, and a group of teenagers sharing a blanket, giggling and enjoying one another's company.

Moving to this area of town was the best decision you ever made. You forgo the vision of the horizon and lie back on your towel, staring straight into the sky. You start to remember the life you left behind, the man you were once hopelessly in love with, the house you once shared. As you picture the outline of your ex-fiancé's jaw and his green eyes, your heart begins to sink. You try to think of something else, and in that process you fall into a light sleep.

Startled by a dream that evoked way too much memory, you wake up an hour later to a dark and deserted beach. You practically jump out of your skin—from both remembering your dream, and the shock of being asleep outside and utterly alone—and start gathering up your belongings.

As you shake out your towel and fold it up, you notice two men—one with dark hair, the other blond—walking toward you at a rather quick pace. You can't make out their faces so you don't know if they might be neighbors.

"Hey gorgeous, what are you doing here all by your little self?" the blond one calls out. They are now almost in front of you. You hug your towel and beach bag tighter to your chest and start to panic.

"Excuse me, guys, I'm just going home." You start walking away and they follow you, almost stepping on the back of your heels.

"I don't think you're going anywhere," the blond man says, moving in front of you and pushing you down to the sand. As you start to scream, his friend grabs your hands and holds them down behind your head while the blond one starts coming down on top of you.

What do you do?

Self-Defense Techniques

When you are pushed down to the ground in an attack, you have an opportunity you probably don't realize. After your attacker has pushed you down, what does he have to do? He has to come down on the ground to your level in any attempt to rape you, hit you, or carry out any other physical violence. This is a probable rape scenario, so the attacker *has* to do something to complete the rape. There will inevitably be an opportunity where his hands will be busy either undoing his pants or undressing you—and that is the moment you need to strike. The key in this type of situation is playing the waiting game. Fussing around and trying to escape without having a plan is just going to deplete you of your energy and make you extremely fatigued.

As far as picking your attacker, it is best to fight against the one who has initiated this move and is closing in on you . . . specifically, the one who is getting on top of you.

- Once you find your opportunity to strike as your attacker is nearing you, you can use both your feet to strike him in the pelvis or throat.
- Alternatively, you can take your left or right foot and wrap it around the opposite ankle of your other leg. Using both of your legs intertwined together, kick out and strike your attacker in the knee to break his leg.
- Once you've defended yourself against the first attacker, you should be able to pull your hands free from the other guy. In fact, he'll have to release you; he's not just going to sit there holding your hands. You've shown you're not an easy target, and you've drawn attention—he doesn't want to get caught.
- Get up, run, and get help.

If you have, or can gain, the use of your hands and arms, here are some options using these natural weapons:

- As the attacker is drawing near to you, it is highly likely that his face will be right in front of yours. As his faces closes in, take the eyes, strike the throat, or cup his ears to give you an escape route.
- If you decide to strike the throat, position your hand into a shuto strike. Don't forget to tuck in your thumb to make your hand as rigid as possible. Strike the throat with your hand in a horizontal position, perpendicular to his throat. If your other hand is free, you can reinforce your strike by using it to push your striking hand forward. As

you move to strike the throat with your horizontal hand, take your other hand and use its fleshy edge to vertically strike your horizontal strike. You can also use the web of your hand to crush his throat.

- If you have both hands, you can cup your attacker's ears and quickly clap your hands against them to blow out his eardrums.
- Run and get help.

Multiple-Attacker Scenario #4:
The Scam

You are so thankful the conference is almost over. Although you are nothing less than passionate about your work, there are only so many speakers you can listen to drone monotonously on and on about the finer points of their research and experience. And my goodness, that last guy practically put you to sleep; never mind the fact that you couldn't understand what he was saying. You've never even heard an accent like that in your life!

Your hotel is located only a few miles away, so instead of hailing a cab, you decide to take the tram along the local streets. You figure you can get off a couple of blocks before your destination and get some air, maybe see some local sights. Getting on the tram car in your scrubs is no picnic. You can feel the wind blowing through your blouse, and there are goose bumps all over your arms. Immediately, you regret not bringing your coat; and with the sun setting so quickly, it's getting colder by the minute.

"Jackson Street," the conductor calls out. "Final call for Jackson Street." You know that this street isn't far from the hotel, so you hop off the tram car and start walking through a quiet neighborhood. Ten minutes into your walk, you decide to take a shortcut. Using your trusty navigation skills, you figure it will lead you right to the side door of your hotel. The minute you turn into the side street, you practically collide head-on with a well-dressed, frantic couple in their early thirties running in your direction. There are tears streaming down the woman's face and while the man is trying to console her, he is clearly just as upset.

"Oh, I'm sorry," the man apologizes. "We didn't mean to run into you."

"My baby, my baby!" The woman is in hysterics. As the man draws the woman closer to him with one arm, he starts to tell you, in between sobbing pauses, that their six-year-old daughter is missing and they don't have a mobile phone on them to call the authorities.

The woman continues to wail. "She was right there with us, we just looked away for two seconds, not even! Oh my God, my poor baby!"

You feel terrible. The worst thing that can happen is to lose a child. You can't imagine what you would do if your daughter was missing. "I'll help you guys, I'm so sorry. What can I do? Here, here, take my phone."

As the woman continues to monopolize your attention by her crying and screaming, the man—unbeknownst to you—quietly starts to step around you to face your back. In a matter of seconds, he grabs your hands from behind and draws you closer to him with incredible force.

"What the—" you cry out.

The woman's crying stops immediately and she grabs your purse.

"We're going to have some fun with you tonight," the man says in your ear.

What do you do?

Self-Defense Techniques

- You should start with the guy who is holding your hands behind your back. Position your foot sideways and use the heel of the foot to strike the middle of one of his feet.
- Using your hands, while he is holding on to them, slam them straight back into his groin area.

- Once he is disabled by your strikes, you can strike any part of his body that is a target area: his eyes, throat, or pelvis. If he is doubled over, you can also use your knee to strike him in the face.
- Run and get help.

12

Weapon-Related Attacks

Fight an attacker's weaknesses. Attack his vulnerability.

I haven't spoken about self-defense techniques that can be used when attacked by assailants carrying weapons, so I'm sure you have some questions and, even more so, concerns. Being attacked by a criminal is scary in and of itself, but when a weapon is employed, it becomes that much more intimidating. You are probably wondering how you can reasonably execute your defensive actions if there is a gun pointed at your temple . . . or if your attacker positions a knife blade on your throat, centimeters away from your jugular vein. You are probably thinking that if you were ever held up at an ATM machine, you would rather give the criminal your money than try to physically defend yourself. Believe me, I know and understand your concerns. Students in workshops tell me that defense against weapons is one of the most challenging tasks they face. However, the challenge doesn't necessarily come from physical abilities—or lack thereof; it comes from having an *I-don't-know-if-I-can-do-it* mind-set.

The way to move from that mentality to an *I-believe-I-can* way of thinking is to understand exactly *why* you can do it. Think about it this way. If self-defense against weapons or persons is only effective when the person executing the techniques is bigger than the assailant, then every martial artist would be over six feet tall and weigh 250-plus pounds. It is not size or strength or abilities that you need to be concerned about. Redirect all that energy and focus on technique instead. Your power to fight back comes not from how hard you can punch, but from the technique you use to strike your attacker. Everything that you have learned so far and continue to read about focuses on the best techniques to use in defending yourself. A child or your elderly grandmother can use these techniques just as effectively as a muscular young man.

Yes, employing self-defensive techniques against weapons may seem challenging, but it is definitely not impossible. Besides, what choice do you have? You can either submit to intimidating threats or do something that can save your life.

Using the right techniques coupled with the element of surprise is what will make the following defensive actions effective. An attacker knows that the average person will be frightened—probably emotionally and physically paralyzed—when faced with a weapon. More than likely, the victim will immediately submit to the attacker and do whatever he says out of fear of getting shot or stabbed. So the last thing the attacker is thinking is, *Hmm, she'll probably fight back, so I'll have to watch out when she does.* In effect, you can blindside the attacker if you know what to do in this type of situation. This is how you automatically turn the tables on the attacker in defense because it is the last thing he is expecting. Surprising him buys you time to follow through, complete defensive action, and run!

Let's say you have planned a surprise party for your wife. The party will be at your home and will begin as soon as she walks through the front door from a hard day of work. If she isn't expecting a party, she will be startled out of her mind. If she has a clue that the party is taking place, though, she simply won't be surprised. Same party, same details, but different reactions based on the element of surprise.

Lastly, as mentioned before, when you are attacked by a weapon, you need to assume that the attacker's intent is to use the weapon. If it's there and you can see it, chances are the criminal will use it. And he won't use it to shoot through air; he'll use it to kill you. You must keep that in mind should you ever be attacked with a weapon. Let it fuel your fight to live and enforce your desire to survive.

On a personal note, I know a woman—a former police officer and a former student of mine from Knoxville, Tennessee—who was approached by a man brandishing a knife. Using correct technique, she was able to defend her life and get the weapon away from his hands. She didn't do anything fancy; she used a simple technique similar to the ones you will learn about in the following pages. She survived a possibly lethal attack not because she was stronger or bigger than the attacker, but because she knew what to do.

If you don't remember anything at all about what I've said so far, remember this. Neither your size, nor strength, nor abilities matter when it comes to defending yourself. What you know is what matters. If you know how to get a gun away from someone, you know enough to save yourself. You *can* employ these techniques. Don't be frightened or discouraged because they seem complicated. They are easy to learn and easy to execute.

You can even practice these techniques using plastic knives and toy guns as props. Enlist a friend or family member and try these techniques on them. You'll start to gain an even stronger sense of comfort.

The Window of Opportunity

A weapon is useless when it is not in the hand of the attacker. A gun lying on the ground can't pick itself up and start shooting—but a gun in the hand of someone else can be lethal. So the first thing you need to do is get the weapon away. A weapon is what gives an attacker the upper hand, boosts his confidence, and intensifies his feeling of power. Once he is disarmed, or his gun or his knife are in your control, a chunk of his supposed power dissipates.

In order to isolate a weapon away from an attacker, you need to see it or feel it to determine exactly where it is. In this sense, being in close proximity to a weapon is an advantage. Think about the importance of closing the gap, in general, with an attacker. The same principle applies to a weapon. If you are being threatened by an assailant and he claims he has a weapon but you cannot see it, what can you do about it? Maybe there is a gun or maybe there isn't. You can't effectively defend against something if you don't know that it's there. If a gun is fixed on your neck, however, you can feel it, you can see it, and, therefore, you can disarm your attacker with the techniques described in the scenarios that follow.

But before we look at how to disarm an attacker, you need to remember that it is essential to exercise considerable caution. What do you think your primary concern is in a weapon-related attack? Yes, that's right. You don't want to get shot, hit, or stabbed with the weapon. So depending on where the weapon is positioned on or near your body, you need to know how to maneuver it so you don't get seriously injured. For example, if there is a gun pointed directly at the side of your head, you need to get your head away from the weapon's line of fire so you don't get shot. Techniques will be demonstrated below for those types of situations.

KEY DEFENSES AGAINST WEAPON ATTACK

- Clear your body from the weapon's line of fire or angle of attack.
- Stabilize and control the weapon.
- Attack the attacker.

Weapon-Related Scenario #1:
At the ATM

You're meeting your friend for dinner in about thirty minutes. It's your first evening social event in about six months, since the birth of your little girl. The night out is a well-deserved break and you're anxious to try out the new tapas place everyone keeps talking about. Not to mention the excitement of finally dropping those last ten persistent pounds so you can show off your figure in your newly purchased little black dress.

Driving on the main road, you realize you don't have a dime on you. Yikes, you hate traveling without any cash. Luckily, your bank has a local branch not far away. It'll only take you about an extra ten minutes to hit the ATM. Although you are irritated at having to make a stop, which will ultimately make you late, you figure you don't have much of a choice.

Pulling into the bank's parking lot, you are disappointed to see a sign on the drive-through ATM that reads BROKEN MACHINE. SEE TELLER OR INSIDE ATM. Now you actually have to get out of the car. Grumbling under your breath, you park the car, hop out, and walk into the bank's foyer. At least there's not a line, you think as you hastily plug your card into the machine and start to punch in your code and request. The machine makes its theatrical sounds and spits out your cash. As you wait for your receipt, you feel something cold and hard digging into the back of your little black dress.

"You're coming with me," a gruff voice growls as he shoves the blunt metal object farther into your back.

What do you do?

Self-Defense Techniques

As I already discussed, your preliminary objective is to get the gun away. Remember that your response is going to happen very fast; your whole defense will take place in a matter of seconds. These moves may sound complex the first time you read them, but remember you want to practice this reaction until it's second nature. Here's what you can do:

- First, put your hands up in a surrender position and say something along these lines to your attacker: "Hey, I'll do whatever you want, I just don't want to get hurt." Doing this will indirectly tell your attacker that you (1) don't want any trouble; (2) don't want to get hurt; and (3) understand he is in control. When you lift your arms in this position, it also gives you a way to free up and expose your hands so you can move into a defensive action when it is least expected. Remember, don't make eye contact, and stand slightly sideways. So when you do move in on him, he will be completely surprised. Now put your right leg back, pivot fast to the right, and move into your attacker. You are turning into him to initially move the gun away and to close the gap.
- As you move to face your attacker, your right elbow moves with you and simultaneously pushes the gun away from your back.
- With your left hand, grab the top of the attacker's hand that is holding on to the gun so that your thumb is on top of his thumb. Place your right hand underneath his hand. Both of your hands should be covering his weapon hand. Turn the weapon into him once you gain control of his hand. You don't want the gun to face you!
- To finish this move, you should take him down to the ground. Here's how. As you are still holding on to his hand, take your left leg and start to pivot it back in order to turn around. You want your back to face his front, mirroring your original position at the ATM. As you

pivot, move your body down to the ground while still holding on to him. Because you have control over his body, it will automatically come down with yours. Keep controlling the weapon. Once he is on the ground, take your knee and hold his head in place with it. Then take your hand and either peel the weapon away from him or shoot him in the leg.

- While the gun is in your hand, assess your surroundings. Check around to see if there are any other assailants lurking in the background.
- Run and get help.

Weapon-Related Scenario #2:
Retail Robbery

"Pack of Marlboro Lights, please," mumbles a teenager who sports a bad case of acne.

You sigh. There is no way this kid looks eighteen. You ask him for identification, which he provides, and you subsequently decide it's valid. The boy gives you exact change for the cigarettes and goes on his merry way while you ruminate about the bad habits teenagers are starting at such young ages.

It's eleven o'clock at night and your shift at the convenience store ends in about an hour. Your feet hurt from standing up all day, and your head hurts from the stale smoke that pours in the store whenever someone swings it open. You want to go home. *One more hour,* you think, *just one more hour.*

As you flip through the latest issue of *People* magazine and grab a peppermint candy from the bucket on the counter, you notice a dark shadow advancing toward you.

When your eyes leave the pages of the magazine and look upward, they greet a big, tall woman dressed in black and wearing a ski mask. Only her cold, lifeless eyes are exposed, and they stare straight into yours. But what catches most of your attention is the barrel of the gun that is cocked about three inches away from your forehead.

"Money. Now. I'll shoot you," the woman blurts out. Her head keeps twitching slightly to both sides of her body, and her hands are shaking. It is clear she is on some type of drug.

"I'll shoot you, you little punk, I'll shoot you."

What do you do?

Self-Defense Techniques

What is the one thing you don't want to happen? That's right, you don't want to get shot in the face or the head. So, since you are staring head-on at the barrel of the gun, the first thing you need to do is to get your face and head away from the gun's line of fire.

- Move your head in either direction, left or right, away from the gun. Do this in a subtle, nondramatic motion so your move is not telegraphed. Don't let your upper body move in the same direction; keep it still and have all movement come from your head and neck.
- Step in toward the assailant with your right foot, using your body weight to help catapult your next move. How far you can step toward the assailant depends on how much counter space lies between you and her. Just move toward her as much as possible; most counters aren't that wide.
- Take both of your hands and put them on her hands; your thumbs should be positioned underneath her hands. Slide your hands up toward the barrel of the gun. The barrel should now be facing toward the ceiling.

- With both of your hands on the gun, slam the gun forward into the attacker's face.
- Once you slam the gun, take one of your hands (with your palm facing the attacker), grab the barrel of the gun, and peel it out of her hand, away from your body. Now the gun is in your hands.
- Run and get help.

Weapon-Related Scenario #3:
Carjacked

"Hey Laura, it's me. I tried to call you before, but you didn't pick up. Where were you? Where are you? Call me back as soon as you get this message. Seriously, where are you? It's almost nine thirty at night. Are you on a date? Call me!"

Sitting in your car in the grocery store parking lot, you hit the END button on your mobile phone and groan. Your sister's voice sounded much too suspicious and caustic; it made her seem even more melodramatic than usual, if that's possible. Although you had heard the phone ring several times before, both of your hands were full of shopping bags, and even if you'd put them down, it would have been impossible to find the phone in your huge purse. *Gotta clean the bag out,* you remind yourself.

You lean back in the driver's seat and stare straight ahead through the windshield. You only need a few moments before you call your sister back. It's a hot day, so you start your engine and roll down the window to get some air. Breathing deep, you pick up your phone and start dialing her number.

In that same instant you see a dark shadow brush past your car and feel something hard and cold against your temple. A man stands right beside the driver's door and has put his gun against the side of your head. You freeze and automatically drop your phone to the ground.

"Move over," he says as he digs the barrel of a gun deeper into your skin. "I'm getting in."

What do you do?

Self-Defense Techniques

There are two types of self-defense techniques that can be utilized in this type of situation, depending on whether your car engine is on or off.

Let's say your car is on and is stationary in the park position. Here is what you can do:

- When you are attacked with a weapon, the number one thing you don't want to have happen is to get shot. You can physically defend yourself against a human being, but things get more challenging when a weapon is aimed directly at you. When you see a gun aimed at the side of your head, immediately move your head straight back to avoid being in the line of fire. If you are sitting in your car, your head does not normally rest on the back of the headrest; there are usually a few inches between the back of your head and the headrest. When you need to get your head out of the way of the line of fire, move your head all the way back to the headrest, or, if you don't have one, far back as possible. Your first priority is getting your head out of the way.
- Using your left hand, grab whichever of the attacker's hands is holding the gun. Firmly grip his wrist with your hand, so your thumb is tightly pressed to the side of his wrist.
- While holding on to his wrist, move his arm to the area of your car between the inside roof of the car and the top of the open window.
- Put the car in gear and drive off still holding on to his wrist. Most likely, he will not want to be dragged down the street and will let go.
- Keep driving and get help.

If your car is not turned on, here's what you can do:

- Put your head back to avoid being in the line of possible fire as mentioned above.
- Raise your left arm upward in an L-shaped block position and strike whichever of the attacker's arms is holding the gun. This maneuver will move the gun away and expose his face.
- Strike his eyes or his throat or both.
- Start the car and drive away.
- Get help.

Weapon-Related Scenario #4:
Strangled

Sometimes, visiting the in-laws can be anything but a picnic. More like a horror flick, to be exact. Here you are, visiting your wife's needy parents, your sister-in-law, her snobbish husband, and their obnoxious, rebellious, and bratty five-year-old twin boys. It's only one week until Christmas, you haven't gotten a restful night of sleep since Easter, and instead of diminishing, it seems your Christmas list is growing by the hour. So what a great excuse to head to the mall . . . alone . . . no one to talk to, no one to complain about, no one to tend to. Just you, a burgeoning Christmas list, and a couple of credit cards.

Four hours, five shopping bags, and three maxed-out credit cards later, you head to the parking garage to find your car. Twice already, you've heard a voice come over a loudspeaker reminding you that the mall will be closing in ten minutes . . . and then five. Once you get to the third floor of the garage, you draw a complete blank as to which section you parked your car in. You tried to play the letter association game, but can't figure out if it was level L for your wife, Lynette, or level G, using your son Gary's name as a reminder. Frustrated, you try L.

Finally, you spot your shiny SUV jutting out of its parking space a few hundred feet away, beckoning you home. Breathing a sigh of relief, you head toward it. *Click-click.* You stop suddenly. Footsteps, you wonder? Did you hear anything? Hmm, probably your imagination.

You press the UNLOCK button on your key chain, and the horn beeps once as the doors unlock themselves. Suddenly, without warning, a piece of rope is thrown over your neck and someone is pulling the end pieces tight in an attempt to strangle you. Your bags immediately fall from your hands as the rope gets tighter and tighter.

What do you do?

Self-Defense Tactics

As you've read before, when attacks happen from behind and you cannot see your assailant, it is best to turn into him so his target areas are exposed and available for you to strike.

- First, figure out which way your body can move. If you can't move to the left, you should be able to move to the right, and vice versa. After deciding on the direction to move, step over his foot in that direction and turn your upper body toward him.
- Immediately after turning to face him, strike his pelvis with the heel of your hand. Remember to pull back immediately after striking the pelvis. If you have easy access to his throat or eyes, take those as well.
- Turn completely around and drop down to the ground. Take him down by grabbing the inside of his ankles with the inside of your palms. Pull them toward you.
- Run and get help!

Weapon-Related Scenario #5:
Jumped from Behind

It's a late afternoon on the day after Thanksgiving. Most of the college kids have left campus to spend the holidays with their families. Thanks to the three term papers you needed to get done, you were one of the unlucky ones who had to spend most of the holiday weekend on campus. You've realized that deciding to go to college close to home is a mixed blessing. While your parents have finally forgiven you for not coming home every weekend, there was no excuse for Thanksgiving Day. Who wants to spend turkey day alone eating cold pizza and drinking Diet Coke, anyway?

With the holiday now over, Friday finds you back on campus . . . slaving over mounds of books, lab reports, and notebooks. On a bright note, you've made significant progress without the twenty-four-hour chatter, laughter, and partying that goes on in your sorority house. Glancing at your watch, you realize you have time for one last, quick trip to the library—and the only running bus on campus leaves in about twenty minutes. You pack up your books and head out the door.

The walk to the bus stop is cold and lonely. The campus looks like a scene out of an old Western movie. You almost expect tumbleweeds to start rolling around in the empty streets. You reach the bus stop, look at your watch, and realize you've grossly miscalculated. You have an extra twenty minutes before the bus is expected to pull up. You pull out your biology textbook and start flipping through the pages.

As you start reading about nerve impulses, you feel a strange sensation behind you. Something or someone is there. In an instant, you see a shadow of a person leap right out of nowhere, and you turn just enough to see a flash of metal in his hand before you are grabbed from behind.

The flat side of a long, shiny knife presses into the right side of your throat as a strong arm pulls around the left side of your body, clutching your left shoulder and chest area.

"Don't move," a raspy voices bellows in your ear.

What do you do?

Self-Defense Techniques

The number one thing you need to remember is you want the knife away from your throat. The worst thing that can happen is having your throat sliced, which could of course be fatal. So your mission is to get the blade away from your throat.

- The closest body part you have to the knife is your right shoulder. Move your right shoulder up toward your right ear. Tuck in your chin and turn your head to the right at the same time. This will move the knife so the blade is not aimed at your throat. It will now be aimed at empty space.
- At the same time, take your left hand and bring it over his knife-holding hand. Grab his wrist with your left hand, making sure your thumb has a firm grip on his wrist.
- As you hold on to his wrist, turn around and step into him with your left foot. As you step into him, take your free hand and put it over your other hand. Now both of your hands are holding on to his knife hand.
- Using both of your hands as you face him, turn the knife around so it is facing him and strike him with it.
- Run and get help.

Weapon-Related Scenario #6:
Confronted by a Knife

You can't stop smiling. You can't stop blushing. You can't stop giggling, daydreaming, or saying his name over and over in your head. *Maybe he's the one*, you wonder. *Maybe this is finally it!* You're in love and you don't care who knows. You're thirty going on sixteen and, best of all, you get to see him tonight.

You have the perfect night planned. A five-course meal, an expensive bottle of Merlot, and an outfit destined to command his attention for the entire evening. You walk briskly down Thirty-third Street, only a few blocks away from your brownstone, but it feels like it's taking an eternity. The sun is setting and your heart is racing in anticipation of your date. Your heels click on the sidewalk in a steady beat and you start speeding up just a little. *Click-click-click.* As you turn the corner to make a right onto your block, you almost run head-on into a guy turning the corner in your direction.

"I'm sorry," you mumble and try to move around him. What you really are thinking is, *Please get the heck out of my way; I have to cook dinner for the father of my future children.*

He starts shifting his body back and forth, mirroring your movements so you cannot physically pass him. You step to the left, he moves with you. You step to the right and he matches your position.

"Hey, I said, excuse me," you exclaim, using a strong and loud tone.

He continues to be mute, snickering slightly. While he is staring at you, you notice he is fumbling for something in his pocket. You hear the click of what you imagine is a switchblade.

"Where are you going, pretty lady?" he snarls as he flicks the blade up to the right side of your neck using his right hand. "*I* don't think you're going anywhere." You can feel the edge of the blade digging deeper into your skin. Your heart jumps to your throat.

What do you do?

Self-Defense Techniques

Remember, the knife has to go. You need to disarm your assailant.

- Take both of your hands and place them over his knife-wielding hand. Be sure both of your thumbs are directly on top of his thumb. At the same time, move your neck out of the way of the knife blade.
- Once you have a grip over his hands, move the knife farther away from your neck. You may think that you don't have the strength to do this, but you will be able to because of the technique involved. Remember, it's technique, not brute force.
- Now you can do a couple of things. While still holding on to and having control of his knife hand, turn it back into him and strike his chest using his own weapon.

13

Attacks
in Your Home

A home is a haven. Your safe place. Its four walls are meant to protect you, provide you with comfort, and maintain your security. You're a stickler for locking your doors and your windows to reinforce your security. You may even have an alarm system installed or own a big, scary dog that warns you of possible intruders.

Home break-ins occur, however, and criminals are not always content with leaving only with your plasma TV or a diamond ring. The necessity to protect yourself doesn't stop when you are finally safe and sound within your home. In the next pages, you'll read about scenarios that occur in home intrusions and learn how you can use self-defense to survive.

Home Invasion Scenario #1:
Surprised in the Kitchen

Should you double up your mortgage payments or pay off the Sears bill this month? Did your husband take care of balancing the checkbook like he promised?

You soak your hands into the sudsy waters that fill up the kitchen sink. God, you hate washing the dishes, but with the dishwasher broken, you don't have much of a choice. What lies heaviest on your mind, however, is not the plethora of pots and pans you must scrub—it's bills. *Bills*—a five letter word that has created an overwhelming amount of stress and a necessity for financial creativity. Why on earth did you choose to take on this responsibility when you and your husband got married? And with such enthusiasm? *My goodness,* you think, *what a mistake!*

Rinsing your kitchen sink clean, you hear some noises coming from your garage. "Tim," you call out. No answer. You realize you never heard your husband's car pull into the garage, but he's definitely in there. Probably parked in the driveway, you think. Teddy, your new Jack Russell terrier, starts scratching at the door leading to the garage. In a matter of seconds, the door opens and Teddy starts barking.

Without turning around you say, "Tim, for God's sake, can you please take Teddy out? He's been acting strange all day." No answer.

In the second you turn around to demand a verbal response from your husband, a pair of gloved hands grabs you by your neck from behind. Someone is trying to strangle you.

What do you do?

Self-Defense Techniques

- When you are grabbed from behind, the one thing you always want to do is turn right around and into your attacker. Remember, close the gap. As with other attacks from behind, you first want to figure out which way your body can move. If you can't move to the left, you should be able to move to the right, and vice versa. After deciding on the direction to move—to the right, let's say—put your weight on your left leg. Now take your right leg and bring it back, turning to step around his opposite foot to face him. In this example, your body is rotating clockwise to face him, so take your right leg and step over his left. (If your body were rotating counterclockwise, you'd use your left leg to step over his right foot.)

- As you turn, you can use whichever arm is on the side that you're turning to loosen his grip around your neck. Move your arm (in this case, the right arm) up in an L-shaped position toward his arm. As you whip around, strike his arm so (1) his grip on you is loosened, and (2) his body is exposed.
- Now that you have access to his target areas, use your left hand to strike his throat in a shuto strike.
- Another option is to strike the pelvic region immediately after striking his arm to loosen the grip.
- Now that you have weakened him, finish off your self-defense techniques by taking him down. Drop down to the ground so your head is facing the lower half of his body. Then place both of your palms on the inside area of each of his ankles. With force, pull his ankles toward you.
- Run and get help.

Home Invasion Scenario #2:
The Delivery

What a luxury. A rainy Saturday afternoon with nothing to do except read, give yourself a manicure, or do absolutely nothing. Nothing at all. You smile to no one in particular, plop yourself on your comfy chocolate suede couch, and power on your entertainment center. *What am I in the mood for?* you wonder. *There's a* Sex and the City *marathon on . . . nah, too much redundant sex talk and martinis.* Your hum-drum suburbia life is a poor match against the city sophisticates. How about some classic 1980s movies about teen angst? *Breakfast Club? Sweet Sixteen?* Nah, reminds you of how much older you're getting. Documentary on serial killers on the Court TV channel? You laugh out loud. On a cozy Saturday afternoon? Not in your life.

You settle on watching old reruns of *CSI* and marvel at Nick Stokes's boyish good looks. "For goodness' sake," you say out loud, "he's younger than my little brother." You continue watching.

The rain trickles down in a steady march, creating a soothing soundtrack for a little nap . . . a power nap, you decide, that will give you the energy you need to clean out your kitchen cupboards, catch up on your e-mail, or do something more exciting, like plucking your eyebrows. As you start dozing off, Nick Stokes's voice seems farther and farther away. And then you're asleep.

There's a sharp knock at the door. "Wha—" you sleepily exclaim. As you struggle to fully wake up, you swing your legs off the couch and start walking toward the door. You peer through the windowpanes in the front door and immediately perk up. A flower delivery person! Wow!

You open the door, and a charming young man greets you. His eyes pore over a pad in his hand and then meet yours. "Kara Jones?" he asks, confirming your identity.

"Yes, that's me," you respond. "Oh my goodness, who are they from?"

The young man shrugs and hands you his pad to sign, confirming receipt of the flowers. "I don't know, ma'am, it should say on the card."

As you try to balance the pad on your forearm to sign, he pushes you inside the house with incredible force. The flowers he was holding crash to the marble tiled foyer. In a matter of seconds he grabs your neck, slams the front door, and shoves you against it. Now both his hands are squeezing your throat so tightly you think you might pass out at any second.

What do you do?

Self-Defense Techniques

His hands are around your neck, and you are facing him. While you clearly have no mobility around your neck and throat area, what part of your body is free? Your arms—which are the most important extremity you have to strike with. As the attacker is choking you, there is a measurable distance between where his hands are around your neck and where his shoulders and arm area begin. This is your greatest opportunity to use. Here's what you can do.

- Step in with your right foot. Take your right hand and move it under his arms, toward his throat. Strike the throat.
- Alternatively, you can go for the eyes. Step in with your right foot. Take both of your hands and move them underneath his arms, up toward his face. Strike his eyes.
- After you have struck a target area on his body to weaken him, finish up the moves by fully weakening the power in his arms. Position both of your hands in a shuto strike—thumbs in, fingers tight. Place them right in the middle of the inside area of his elbows and strike down into his flesh. Both of his arms will drop.
- Now you have to do something so he no longer has you cornered with your back to the door. With the palm of your left hand, grab the back of his head in a cupping motion. Follow through by placing your right hand over your left hand. As you move your hands to bring him forward toward the door, move toward the right so you are not between the attacker and door. Slam his head into the door as your hands are still cupped behind his head.
- Run! Run to a neighbor's house to get help. While you can stay inside your home to grab your phone and call 911, your best bet is to run away from it. If your cell phone is somewhere within reach, take

it with you and run. Escape to a safe place, a neighbor's home, or into your car (if you have time to grab your keys) and get help.

Home Invasion Scenario #3:
The Enraged Ex

Ugh, I need to start marking my keys, you mumble to yourself as you try to manipulate each of the twenty keys on your key holder into the keyhole area. *Where did all these keys even come from?* you wonder. Your boyfriend probably put duplicates of all of his keys on your key chain. Ai! At last, the fourth one works. Great. You slam and lock the door shut behind you. As you stumble into the house, feeling very exhausted, you start repeating your reminders to mark your home key. "Mark home key," you say out loud, "mark home key." You drop your gym bag and laptop bag on the floor and open the drawer on your hall bureau. "Mark home key, mark home key." To your satisfaction, you find a blue permanent marker and furiously begin to color the metal object.

Satisfied, you smile. Home key marked. Hallelujah! Your stomach rumbles, reminding you it's past dinnertime. Walking to the kitchen, you realize the grocery shopping hasn't been done this week, through no fault of your own. Your roommate, Carl, isn't one to religiously follow through with his chores, and you always seem to experience the repercussions of his irresponsibility.

You open the fridge. Beer, Red Bull, OJ, two-week-old bread, low-carb pasta from that new hip bistro down the street, and pizza from last night's dinner. Not much of an appetizing cuisine selection. You head toward the pantry closet at the far end of the kitchen to see if you can find something better.

Right before the door to the pantry closet, there is a small enclosed hallway containing stairs that lead to the second floor. As you walk toward the pantry, you get a creepy sensation that someone's watching you. Weird. Maybe Carl's ex-girlfriend Jane is upstairs waiting for him. You can't believe she still has the key to your house . . . she was one crazy chick. She is still convinced you and Carl are more than just roommates, despite the fact that you have a boyfriend and you and Carl have been friends since preschool. You remember how relieved you were when Carl finally dumped her, though she keeps desperately trying to hang around. As you walk into the pantry, you are pulled by your shoulders backward into the arms of a thin, but very muscular woman. It's her. The ex-girlfriend. Jane.

You start to yell, "What the hell are you doing, Jane?" But you almost lose your balance as she grips you tighter and starts screaming out threats that she is going to kill you and Carl.

What do you do?

Self-Defense Techniques

- Use the heel of your foot to stomp on the middle part of her foot or strike her shin with your foot.
- Then close the gap and face her. Figure out which way your body can move. If you can't move to the left, you should be able to move to the right, and vice versa. Step to the side and turn your upper body to face her.
- Once you are facing her, strike her pelvis or throat.
- You can then take her feet out from under her by dropping low to the ground, grabbing the insides of her ankles, and pulling them toward you.
- Run out of the house and get help.

14
Domestic-Violence-Related Attacks

This would never happen to me. The idea of being attacked by a loved one is something most people do not want to read about, let alone think about. The sad truth, however, is that it happens . . . and to such a considerable degree that it does merit the inclusion of this chapter. While domestic violence victims can be both male and female, the majority are women. For that reason, this chapter will focus primarily on situations involving women needing to employ self-defense techniques. Of course, these techniques can be carried out by men who find themselves in similar situations. The bottom line is that they work, whether executed by a man or a woman.

You've learned that self-defense means saving your own life by defending yourself against someone trying to harm or kill you. You've learned the vital target areas you can strike to severely maim an attacker. In using your defenses, you understand that your actions are used to severely debilitate an attacker. You have no mercy; you don't have the time or the luxury for it. In this chapter, however, because the attackers are people with whom you have an intimate relationship, your intent for self-defense is to control the situation and take away the supposed power and intimidation of the other party, not severely injure him. You don't want to necessarily blind him by striking his eyes, but you want to physically defend yourself and express your refusal to be manhandled, pushed around, or threatened. You need to control these types of violent incidents and, specifically, the person trying to harm you.

The scenarios you will read below relate solely to a first-time offense. If you are currently involved in an abusive relationship, you don't need me to tell you that you need to get out. The only method of self-defense in a continually abusive situation is to leave that relationship. In that sense, these scenarios will not necessarily aid a person involved in intimate violence unless she is prepared to permanently terminate the relationship.

Domestic Violence Scenario #1: *A Drunken Husband*

The door slams and its sound echoes throughout the entire house. The floor shakes slightly and your heartbeat quickens. *Oh great,* you think, *he's had a bad day at work and he's angry again.*

You hear your husband walking toward the bedroom where you sit on your bed organizing the photos from your first anniversary party.

The stench of alcohol and stale smoke drifts through the bedroom. You start to feel queasy and gently pat your protruding stomach, sighing.

Your husband pokes his head through the doorway, sporting a five o'clock shadow and glassy eyes. His speech is slightly slurred.

"Where's dinner? You said you were making something sshpecial. Wheresit?" He leaves the door frame and starts making his way toward you. The look in his eye frightens you; you've never seen anything quite like it. He's had severe mood swings recently, but the doctor said the medication should be evening them out.

"Honey, it's almost ten. There's leftovers in the fridge." You rub your stomach again, slowly slide off the bed, and plant your feet firmly on the ground. Your husband inches his way as close to you as possible. You're almost positive you will start to upchuck from the putrid beer smell.

"Whereshh dinner?" he continues to scream. "Where's dinner, you lazy—" He gives you a slight shove with his right hand, and his left hand follows suit with a stronger amount of pressure. You lose your balance and fall back onto the bed. You fear for your life. It's the moment you swore would never happen.

What do you do?

Self-Defense Techniques

Close the gap. I can't repeat this often enough. This method of initial self-defense is necessary to control or debilitate an attacker who is trying to harm you. The extra physical space between you only adds time and space that will (1) make you more afraid; (2) make you feel more vulnerable; and (3) essentially waste time that can be better spent taking control of the situation. To close the gap, either get up (depending on your physical location) or move toward him. Here's what you can do after closing the gap.

- First, weaken him by focusing on one of his target areas. You can strike the area between his upper lip and his nose, for instance.
- Take an open palm and put it over his face. The heel of your hand should be near his chin. Grab his face in that manner and continue to take him down, firmly gripping his face.
- At the same time, firmly grab the back of his head and hold tight while taking his body down to the ground. Step back with the same leg as the hand that you put behind his head and keep gripping his head with both of your hands as you take him down to the floor. The most important thing to remember is to use the correct footwork while you are doing this.
- Run and get help.

Domestic Violence Scenario #2:
Escaping a Headlock

"I'm not signing the divorce papers and that's final." Your soon-to-be ex-husband makes the declarative statement with great conviction and throws the documents in your face. His face is flushed with anger, and his jaw is clenched tight. You don't even flinch. You knew this wasn't going to be easy and that he would probably start flipping out in one of his uncontrollable rages. That is the main reason you had served him with the divorce papers in the first place.

You had been married for about five years when he got laid off, starting a yearlong domino effect of continual disaster. He started drinking heavily and became verbally and emotionally abusive. Medication didn't work. Nor did counseling, extra patience, self-help books, or anything else you tried. The last straw was when he gave you a black eye. It was the first and last time he ever raised a hand toward you and it shocked you to no end. You understood the marriage wasn't worth saving and you ultimately had no choice but to leave.

You've been staying with friends and rarely leave the house by yourself for fear of running into him. You don't want to take any chances. But there he is, on a bright Sunday afternoon, standing on the porch waving divorce papers he wants nothing to do with. Obviously, you wouldn't have opened the door if you knew he was there. But you had to get to the mailbox and he practically jumped onto the porch out of nowhere, eventually forcing his way into your friends' home with his brute strength.

You aren't going to let him see you afraid, though. "Stay away from me," you warn him. "I'm calling the police." As you calmly pick up your cell phone, keeping your eyes on him the entire time, he rushes toward you, slaps the phone out of your hand, and puts you in a headlock.

"You're calling nobody," he snarls.

What do you do?

Self-Defense Techniques

Below are defensive actions against any headlock positions.

- When you are put in a headlock and are positioned slightly to the side of your attacker, your arms will be dangling at your sides. So while your head and neck region is rendered practically useless, you still have free and full use of your arms. Take your right arm and move it around to the front of his left side.
- Bring your hand to the side of his neck toward his face. Take the palm of your hand and strike the area between his nose and upper lip. Doing this will get his face and head back.
- You will automatically create distance between his body and yours, thus exposing major target areas on his body.
- A great target area to strike is his pelvic area. Use a hammer blow by making a fist and hitting his pelvis with the fleshy part of your fist, where your pinkie is.
- Run and get help.

Domestic Violence Scenario #3:
An Abusive Boyfriend

You have been dating Mark for about three months. He has an irresistible charm and witty humor—the two exact things that attracted you to him in the first place. His good looks are definitely a great fringe benefit: He's six feet two and two hundred pounds of solid muscle—arms, legs, and abs of steel. In the few weeks you've known him, he's been generally well mannered with the exception of a few temper tantrums, which you excused for whatever reasons. Now the red flags start reappearing in your head, though, and you realize your foolishness.

You and Mark just finished dinner at a local restaurant and have returned to his apartment. Your friend Joe, married to one of your best friends, called your mobile phone twice during dinner. When the phone rings a third time, Mark grabs the phone from you, sees Joe's name, and blows up in a fit of unnecessary rage.

"Mark, I'm sorry, I just—" You attempt to calmly reason with him and back your way toward the front door. What you want to do is book it out of his apartment.

"What, are you sleeping with this guy?" His eyes are wild.

"There's no reason to raise your voice. You're being silly. You're acting jealous for no reason."

Mark fumes and starts waving his hands around furiously. "I'm jealous? I'm jealous? The guy calls you fifty times in ten minutes. What am I supposed to do? How could you do this to me?"

You start getting genuinely scared at this point. Mark gets more volatile by the second and is now calling you every name in the book. He raises his hand, about to slap you across the face. "You little—"

"Stop it," you yell and block his hand with yours. He looks surprised but immediately takes both of his hands and places them on your neck.

"I'll teach you a lesson," he says and starts to strangle you.

What do you do?

Self-Defense Techniques

- Step in with your right or left leg. Cup your hands and use them to slam his ears.

- Go down to the ground and take him off his feet. Use your hands to grasp his ankles (the palms of your hands facing the inside of his ankles) and pull them toward you to make him lose his balance.
- Run and get help.

Domestic Violence Scenario #4:
A Bad Breakup

Tempers are flaring between you and the guy you have recently broken up with. Two years with him was two years too long. Although you regret the length of time it took to realize how bad the situation really was, you're grateful you actually made the decision. Leaving him was the best thing to do. Things never escalated to a physically violent point, but it was clear the relationship was definitely headed in that direction. And that is something you could never put up with, so you ended it. Finally.

Both of you have very strong personalities, which was both a positive and a negative aspect of your relationship, depending on the situation. Your emotional barometer was always either at a low or an extreme high, and you realized neither of you could depend on the other for stability. It was bad; but you did end it, so there is no problem, right? Wrong.

He shows up at your friend Jill's house where you finished having dinner with her and her husband. As you bid your friends good-bye and walk toward the street, you see his car parked a block ahead of yours. Instead of turning around and going back inside your friends' home, you start walking toward his car, yelling and screaming, fuming with anger.

You knock harshly at his window and say, "What the hell are you doing here? Can't you just leave me alone?"

He jumps out of the car and starts saying how sorry he is. You are not in the mood for his pathetic apologies and you, one more time, tell him to leave you alone. You are emphatic in your tone and in the words you use.

You stare at each for what seems like an eternity, but it is only a second or two. "Look . . ." He begins to reach his hand out to touch your shoulder.

"Don't touch me," you say and take a step backward. He becomes more aggressive, wrapping the front of your shirt around his hand and pulling you closer to him. He starts screaming in your face.

What do you do?

Self-Defense Techniques

- A great advantage you have is that one of his hands is tied up in your shirt. It is not available for him to use to strike you.
- Put your hand over whichever of his hands is grabbing your shirt to control it. When your hand is on top of his, his hand is not going anywhere. You have locked him in.
- Using your free hand, strike his eyes to weaken him.
- Use the same free hand in a shuto position to strike the inside elbow area of his other arm. What this does is weaken his balance, helping you execute a take-down move.
- Take a step back and pull his hand that is still holding on to your shirt downward, taking him down to the ground. Whatever hand you are using to control the attacker's hand, use the same leg to step back with.
- Run and get help.

15

Now What?

So now here you are. Finally, you are eyeing the last few pages of this book. Do you feel empowered? Confident? Knowledgeable? Do you feel ready to handle a physically threatening situation if you came face-to-face with one? Do you believe you truly stand a considerable chance in defending yourself against an attacker? What did you learn that you would have otherwise been ignorant about?

If you flip back to the first chapter, you'll be reminded of the reasons you chose to read this book and the challenges you thought you would face in learning about self-defense. Read your answers and ask yourself:

- Did I learn what I thought I would when I picked up this book?
- Did it answer the questions I had?
- Do those challenges still exist?
- Do I feel more confident in my ability to execute self-defense?

In the spaces below, write down how those initial challenges were overcome through learning about self-defense. You may have thought your petite size would be a sure obstacle against a bigger assailant, for instance, but now you understand why size doesn't matter—mental strength and learning how to fight weaknesses, not strengths, are what fuel effective self-defense.

Challenges I've Overcome

_____

_____

_____

_____

_____

_____

Additionally, what did you learn that surprised you? For example, some people I know are made aware of their general inattentiveness when going about their lives. Before reading this, they had absolutely no idea they hardly paid attention to their surroundings! Others learned about nifty safety tricks to use in their homes that they wouldn't have otherwise known of. List yours below:

Unexpected Lessons I've Learned

_____

_____

_____

_____

_____

_____

_____

Pay Attention

Distractions can be our own worst enemy and can haunt us in almost every aspect of our lives. I've read about one too many car accidents that occurred from drivers being occupied on mobile phones. They were engrossed in deep or entertaining conversation and somehow missed the red light . . . or the stop sign . . . or almost rear-ended the stopped car in front of them at the light.

How many marriages do you know that have ended when one spouse says, "I'm sorry, but I'm not in love with you anymore. I want a divorce," and the other spouse wonders where the warning signs were? Usually, after careful meditation, the red flags were evident, but they were ignored for a multitude of reasons—reasons that never carried more weight than a failing marriage ready to crumble.

Distractions are a constant in our lives because life is in perpetual motion. Unless we are comatose or board ourselves in our bedroom each day, we are involved in different types of emotional, physical, mental, and spiritual experiences. These experiences influence our emotions, and our quality of life is ultimately affected by them to whatever degree we allow. Distractions are commonplace and normal. But what happens when they overwhelm our minds and take up a majority of our thoughts, energies, and emotions? We automatically become vulnerable.

If we're walking down a crowded hallway engulfed with worry about what someone said the other night, we can easily walk right into someone without even seeing him prior to the collision. We are surprised. We are caught off-guard. Because we are not paying attention, we miss important things about life that we should not have missed.

The same principle of being alert applies in the arena of self-defense. We have learned about preventive self-defense, being present when we are in both familiar and unfamiliar surroundings, and need to practice self-safety. Being present means being aware of our environment, paying attention to what's going on around us. It means listening to footsteps that seem to follow on our heels. It means locking our doors and our windows at all times. It means keeping our eyes moving in all directions rather than fixating on a specific spot.

When we don't pay attention as we walk or shop or jog, we risk being vulnerable and being targeted as easy prey. We risk having to use self-defense when we might have been able to walk away and avoid a bad situation entirely. Pay attention; it could just save your life.

Mind Over Matter

What is the number one self-defense weapon available to us? Our minds. William James, one of the first professors to introduce and teach psychology at American universities, once said, "It is our attitude at the beginning of a difficult task which, more than anything else, will affect its successful outcome."

Our beliefs and values originate in the attitudes we create for ourselves. Having the right mental attitude is critical in determining our overall state of well-being. We need to form the right attitude in order to be able to use self-defense effectively and for the right reasons. So what fundamental truths do we need to believe and reinforce in our minds to learn self-defense? Read the following out loud:

- I am a valuable human being.
- I have the right to protect my own life.
- I give myself permission to fight back if I am involved in a life-threatening situation.
- I can physically fight back against a criminal despite his size or strength.

- I can escape a physically volatile attack using mental and physical self-defense.

Investing your mental attitude into these truths will pave the way for effective self-defense. All the muscle and power in the world couldn't weaken a positive and healthy attitude. You must truly believe these statements with your head and with your heart if you want to stand a chance at being victorious.

It is your life that you are responsible to keep, enjoy, participate in, and defend. No one else has a moral, social, and conscious responsibility to be your twenty-four-hour keeper and bodyguard. If you are being harmed, you have no choice but to defend your life.

Your life is yours. It doesn't belong to some stranger who wants to use it to his advantage and on his whims. It doesn't belong to a criminal who happened to target you because you have blond hair. It doesn't belong to an attacker who has had terrible experiences with women and feels he is justified in taking his revenge out on you. It's *your* life—your body, soul, and mind—and it is up to you to make a conscious choice to save it.

What will you do?